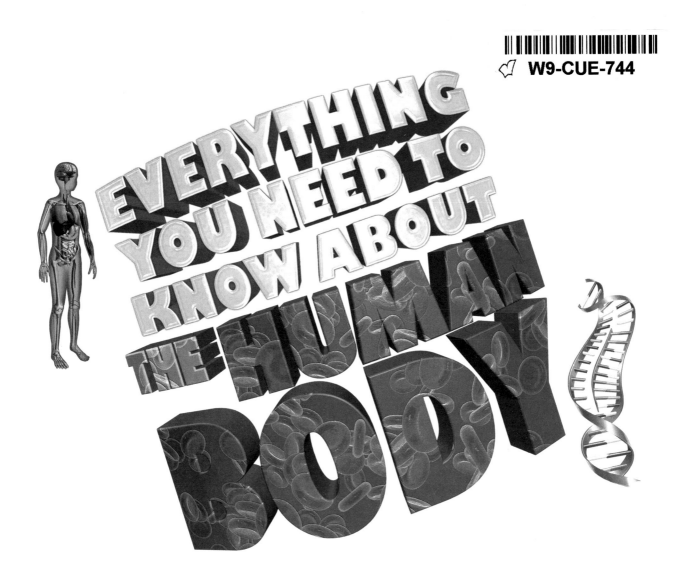

Copyright © Kingfisher 2011
Published in the United States by Kingfisher,
175 Fifth Ave., New York, NY 10010
Kingfisher is an imprint of Macmillan Children's Books, London.

Consultant: Dr. Graham Neale, Imperial College, London

Distributed in the U.S. and Canada by Macmillan,
175 Fifth Ave., New York, NY 10010

First published in hardback by Kingfisher in 2011
This paperback edition published by Kingfisher in 2014

Library of Congress Cataloging-in-Publication data has been applied for.

ISBN: 978-0-7534-7168-5

Kingfisher books are available for special promotions and premiums.
For details contact: Special Markets Department, Macmillan, 175 Fifth Ave.,
New York, NY 10010.

For more information, please visit www.kingfisherbooks.com

Printed in China
9 8 7 6 5 4 3 2 1
1TR/0314/WKT/UG/128MA

NOTE TO READERS

The website addresses listed in this book are correct at the time of going to print.
However, due to the ever-changing nature of the Internet, website addresses and
content can change. Websites can contain links that are unsuitable for children.
The publisher cannot be held responsible for changes in website addresses or content
or for information obtained through third-party websites. We strongly advise that
Internet searches should be supervised by an adult.

Everything You Need to Know About the Human Body

Dr. Patricia Macnair

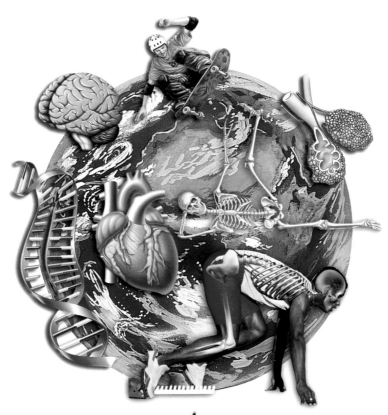

KINGFISHER
NEW YORK

Contents

Food and digestion

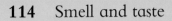

The brain and senses

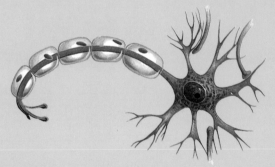

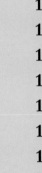

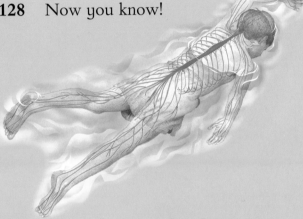

Structure and movement

Using this book

As well as offering a lot of information, this book has many fun ideas in it to help you enjoy it more. There are facts to amaze you, vocabulary notepads to explain words, important questions with fascinating answers, and great activities. Enjoy finding out all about the human body!

VOCABULARY

antibodies
Chemicals that help fight infections

bacteria
Tiny organisms that cause infections

hormones
Chemical messengers sent around the body

▼ Fact box

Look out for these boxes. Each fact box contains interesting information about the subject being described. This fact box is from the chapter called "Structure and movement." You will find it on page 143.

▲ Vocabulary notepad

Sometimes difficult words that need further explanation are used in the text, so there is a notepad especially for this task. This vocabulary notepad is from the chapter called "What makes a human body?" You will find it on page 26.

FOOTPRINT FACTS

Dinosaur footprints left behind in mud or volcanic ash can still be seen today. Scientists study these to figure out which dinosaurs existed in a particular area and how long ago. A few ancient human footprints have been left behind for us to wonder about and investigate, too.

▶ Amazing facts

Look out for the exclamation mark on these boxes. Each "Amazing!" box contains an extraordinary fact. This "Amazing!" box is from the chapter called "Growing and changing." You will find it on page 50.

AMAZING!

Some children start to play a musical instrument when they are just five years old. The famous Austrian composer Wolfgang Amadeus Mozart wrote his first musical pieces at the age of five, by which time he could already play the piano and the violin.

CAN YOU FIND?

1. Someone tasting
2. Someone hearing
3. Someone touching
4. Someone seeing

◀ Can you find?

These features test what you can spot in the pictures. This head-shaped "Can you find?" is from the chapter called "The brain and senses." You will find it on page 106.

▶ Question circle

Everyone has questions they really want to ask. You will find circles with questions and their answers in every chapter. This question circle is from the chapter called "Food and digestion." You will find it on page 83.

WHAT KEEPS FOOD IN THE STOMACH?

The entrance and exit of the stomach are made from powerful muscles, called sphincters, that can close tight or relax to let food through.

CREATIVE CORNER

Where are your organs?

Lie on a large piece of paper and ask a friend to trace around your body. Now draw pictures of the organs mentioned here and see if you can put them in the right places inside your body outline.

▲ Creative corner

The splotch of paint says it all! This is where you can let your creative self run wild. The book is packed with fun experiments and great things to make and try. This creative corner is from the chapter called "What makes a human body?" You will find it on page 21.

▲ You will need

Plain and colored paper and cardboard, glue, scissors, pencils, an eraser, crayons, paints, paintbrushes, toys, building blocks, coins, a ball, gloves, a friend, and yourself!

▼ At the bottom of most of the right-hand pages in the book you will find a useful website. These have been carefully chosen to add to the information on each page.

What makes a human body?

There are more than six billion people
on Earth. We all have similar bodies, yet each
of us is very different. So what is the recipe
for a human? What are we made of,
and what can we do?

We are all different!

Look at your friends and you will see that everyone has the same body parts, such as arms, legs, and a head, but no one is exactly the same. People are tall or short, dark or fair. Each one of us is completely unique.

▶ You usually recognize people you know by looking at their faces. Each person has his or her own special combination of facial features such as curly, dark hair, freckles, and a sassy grin. Even identical twins look slightly different from each other.

▲▼ People look different, and they behave differently, too. Some people love to run around making noise or playing sports, while others are quieter and like to read or daydream. Everyone has a different personality.

CAN YOU FIND?
1. A pair of twins
2. A father and son
3. A grandmother and grandson
4. Two friends

HOW TALL?

Some people grow to be as much as 6.5 ft. (2m) tall. They make good basketball players because they can reach the net easily! However, most adults are 5–6 ft. (1.5–1.8m) tall.

▼ What makes us all different? In every cell in the body, there is a code of instructions called our genes. Genes tell the body how to make or repair itself. We inherit a mixture of genes from our parents, so we often look like them. Other people have different genes, so they look different from us.

AMAZING!

The number of people in the world is increasing at an incredible rate. Every minute that goes by, there are about 180 more people living on Earth. By the end of this century, there may be well over nine billion people on the planet.

INTERNET LINKS: www.sciencemuseum.org.uk/whoami/thingdom.aspx

What the body can do

Humans can control and change the world in ways that no other living thing can. We stand upright on two legs, so our arms and hands are free to carry things and use tools. We also use language to share ideas with one another and pass on knowledge and information.

► Although we cannot run as fast as a cheetah or swim like a dolphin, our bodies are strong and flexible. We can push, pull, bend, stretch, and lift, which allows us to carry anything we need and build our own homes.

CAN YOU FIND?
1. People sharing ideas
2. Someone using a tool
3. A person carrying bricks
4. A man using a hammer
5. Someone bending

▲ Humans have abstract thoughts. This means we can think about things that we cannot actually see or that do not even exist. This allows people to invent new ways of doing things that might make our lives better.

DO ANIMALS FEEL EMOTIONS?
Animals seem to have emotions like joy and fear, but it is difficult to be sure about this because they cannot tell us!

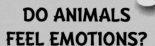

▲ Our intelligent human brains have developed all sorts of systems to help us communicate with one another and get things done more easily. With modern technology, we can see and talk to other people wherever they are in the world.

UNDERSTANDING OURSELVES

Humans are always using their brains to try to find out more about the world. In 1953, scientists answered one of the most important questions about the human body when they figured out what DNA, the recipe for human life, is made of.

Inside the body

brain

lungs

No matter what we look like on the outside, we are all built to much the same pattern inside. Each one of us has the same structures, or organs, that rumble and churn all day long to keep our bodies working as they should.

heart

liver

◀ Just like a busy town, there are all sorts of systems at work in our bodies, doing jobs like taking in food and oxygen and getting rid of waste, as well as carrying out other special tasks.

AMAZING!
We are made of many different chemicals. The average human body contains enough iron to make a nail 3 in. (7cm) long, enough sulfur to kill all the fleas on a dog, and enough carbon to make 900 pencils!

large intestine

small intestine

blood vessels

▶ Deep inside your body is a very hard frame, called the skeleton, which holds the body upright and makes it strong. Along with the muscle, fat, and skin that surround it, the skeleton provides the shape of the body, too.

baby   child   man

HOW WATERY ARE YOU?

Our bodies are mostly made of water. A newborn baby is about 78 percent water, but when he is one year old, he will be only 65 percent water. An adult man is about 60 percent water, but a woman is only 55 percent water.

▶ Your body is full of all sorts of liquids doing important jobs. Juices in your intestines help digest food, blood carries oxygen and food around, urine takes away waste products, and tears clean your eyes.

▶ Your body may feel solid, but there is a lot of gas inside it, too. Your lungs are full of air that you can use to blow out candles or blow up a balloon. If you listen carefully, you might hear gas bubbles gurgling inside your stomach.

15

Cells

Your body is made up of an incredible 100 trillion (that is 100,000,000,000,000!) tiny units called cells. Cells are so small that several thousand would fit on the head of a pin, and you cannot see them without special magnifying equipment called a microscope.

▶ Each cell is surrounded by a protective membrane that is thin and flexible like a plastic shopping bag. Inside this are several tiny structures, including a control center called the nucleus, where your DNA, or genes, is stored.

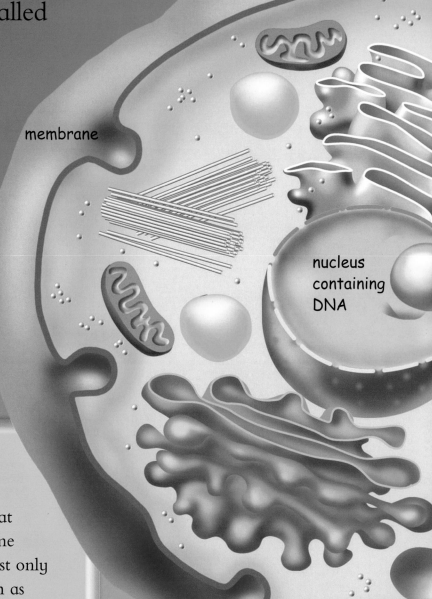

membrane

nucleus containing DNA

AMAZING!

Your body makes new cells all the time to replace old ones that are worn out or damaged. Some cells, such as red blood cells, last only a few weeks, while others, such as nerve cells, may last a lifetime.

▼ There are about 200 different types of cells in the body, all of which have different jobs to do. Some take in nutrients from food in the intestines, and others attack invading germs or make chemical messages to send around the body.

▼ The shape of each cell suits the job it does. Skin cells are flat and form a smooth surface. Blood cells are doughnut shaped to squeeze through narrow arteries and veins. Nerve cells are long and spidery.

VOCABULARY

DNA
A chemical that carries the code for life

membrane
The outer surface of a cell

nucleus
The control center of a cell, where DNA is stored

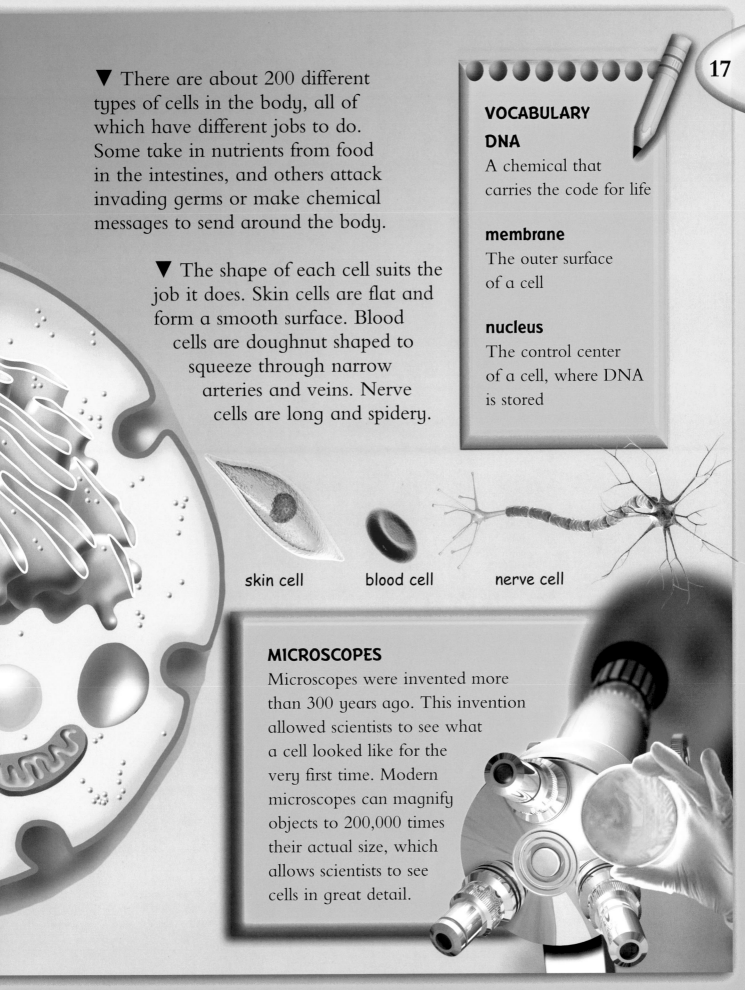

skin cell   blood cell   nerve cell

MICROSCOPES

Microscopes were invented more than 300 years ago. This invention allowed scientists to see what a cell looked like for the very first time. Modern microscopes can magnify objects to 200,000 times their actual size, which allows scientists to see cells in great detail.

INTERNET LINKS: www.sciencemuseum.org.uk/WhoAmI/FindOutMore/Yourbody/Whatdoyourcellsdo.aspx

Tissues

Cells work together in groups to carry out the jobs they do. These groups are called tissues. They are made mostly of one or two particular types of cells, but other types may be needed, too. Nerve tissue, for example, is packed with nerve cells but also contains blood cells and lining cells.

VOCABULARY

biceps
The muscle in the arm that pulls up the lower arm

tendons
The long, tough cords of tissue joining muscles and bones

▲ The stringy tendons you can see on the backs of your hands are made from connective tissue. This type of tissue joins and supports different parts of the body. In the hands, the tendons join the muscles to the bones and help you move your fingers.

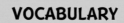

WHAT HAPPENS WHEN TISSUE IS DAMAGED?

Most body tissues can repair themselves. This is called regeneration, and some tissues are better at it than others.

biceps muscle

bone

tendon

▲ The cells in muscle tissue are long and bunched together like a rope. Muscle cells can contract, or get shorter, which helps you move. When you bend your arm, the biceps muscle gets shorter and pulls up the arm bones.

AMAZING!

Some tissues that become damaged or diseased can be replaced with tissues from another person. This is called a transplant. For example, the clear tissue that covers the front of the eye, called the cornea, can be transplanted, and this can help someone see.

◀ Your skin is an example of covering, or lining, tissue. It is made from a flat sheet of cells that forms a barrier, wrapping around and protecting your body. The linings of your mouth and digestive system are also made of lining tissue.

INTERNET LINKS: http://kidshealth.org/kid/htbw/muscles.html

Your organs

Different types of tissues are grouped together to form organs such as your heart and liver. Many organs are like factories, with walls and roofs made from lining tissues and other tissues such as nerves or muscles helping the organ do its work.

brain

▶ Each of your organs carries out a particular job and has a recognizable shape. The stomach, for example, is a J-shaped bag. Some organs, such as the lungs, work as a pair.

lungs

heart

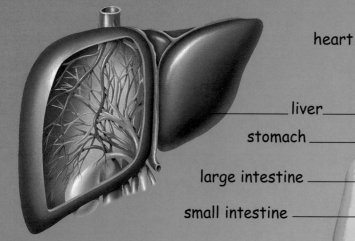

liver

stomach

large intestine

small intestine

▲ The liver is the largest organ in the abdomen. It receives nutrients from the food in your digestive system, brought to it by your blood. It then turns those nutrients into useful substances.

AMAZING!
There are dozens of organs in your body, and it is difficult to live without most of them. In your head alone, there are your eyes, teeth, tongue, nose, and tonsils, to name just a few.

lung ——————

—— alveoli

▶ The brain is an amazing but mysterious organ made mostly of nerve tissue. Shaped liked a huge, wrinkled walnut, it is hidden away inside the thick, protective tissue of the skull.

▲ The lungs are large organs inside your chest, made of stretchy connective tissue. They are like sponges full of millions of tiny, bubblelike spaces, where the gas oxygen is taken into the body.

CREATIVE CORNER

Where are your organs?
Lie on a large piece of paper and ask a friend to trace around your body. Now draw pictures of the organs mentioned here and see if you can put them in the right places inside your body outline.

The skin system

Two or more of your organs may work together as a group, called a system, to carry out jobs related to each other. The outer surface of the body makes up a system whose job it is to protect the body. It includes three organs—the skin, hair, and nails.

▼ The skin is the largest organ in your body. It is packed with millions of tiny structures and carries out many important jobs. It defends the body against harm, controls your temperature, and tells the brain about the world around you.

BACTERIA

Your skin is covered with millions of microscopic bacteria. Most are harmless and may even help the skin keep more dangerous bacteria away.

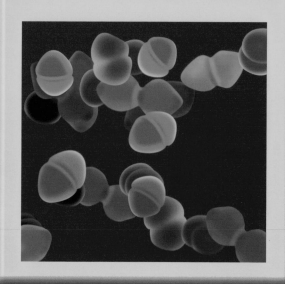

oil gland   hair_____   sensor

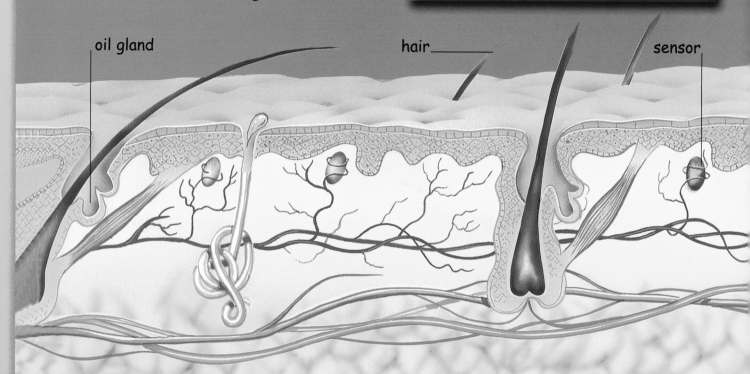

◀ Hair helps protect the body and keep it warm. Some parts of your skin are very hairy, such as the scalp, while others have fine hairs or no hair at all. Some animals, such as cats, are hairy all over.

▼ The skin consists of two main layers. The top layer is waterproof and formed by many flat cells. Beneath it is a layer full of glands making sweat and oil, hair roots, tiny sensors, nerves, and blood vessels.

IS SUNLIGHT GOOD FOR THE SKIN?
The skin needs sunlight to make vitamin D for healthy bones, but too much strong sunlight can burn and damage the skin.

▲ Fingernails and toenails are made of layers of cells packed down hard. They protect the sensitive fingertips and are useful for gripping and scraping. Because the cells are dead, it does not hurt when you cut your nails.

nerve   blood vessel   sweat gland

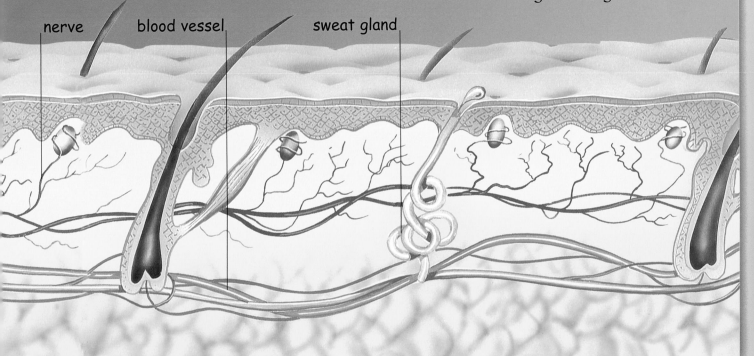

INTERNET LINKS: www.kidsskinhealth.org/kids/index.html

Blood on the move

24

Blood moves around your body all the time, carrying food and oxygen to the tissues and removing waste products. The heart and the blood-carrying tubes called blood vessels together make up the circulatory system.

valve

right side of the heart

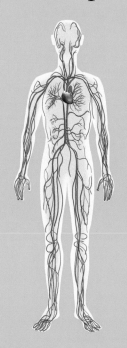

◀ The heart is the pump at the center of this transportation system. With each heartbeat, its muscular walls push blood out through the blood vessels. An adult's heart beats about 70 times a minute, but your heart beats a little faster.

wall of heart made from muscle tissue

AMAZING!

If every blood vessel in your body was laid out end to end, they would stretch for more than 62,000 mi. (100,000km). That is more than twice the distance around the world!

▶ The heart is divided into two sides, left and right. The right side pumps blood to the lungs, where it collects oxygen and turns brighter red. It then returns to the left side of the heart, which pumps it out around the body.

blood vessels

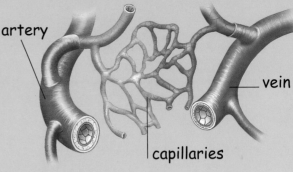

artery

vein

capillaries

WHAT KEEPS BLOOD FLOWING THE RIGHT WAY?

In the heart and veins there are flaps called valves that stop blood from flowing in the wrong direction.

▲ Blood vessels called arteries take blood rich in oxygen to the tissues. There, the blood enters a network of tiny vessels (called capillaries), passes food and oxygen to the cells, and collects waste. Then the blood travels back to the heart through the veins.

left side of the heart

► If you scrape your knee, blood leaks from the damaged blood vessels. It quickly sticks together to form a clot, which seals the vessels and stops them from bleeding any more.

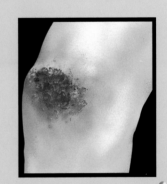

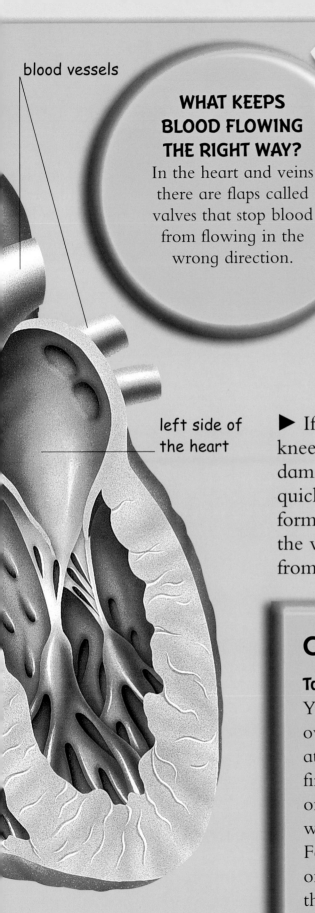

CREATIVE CORNER

Take your pulse!

You can feel your own circulation system at work by placing two fingers on the outer edge of your wrist, below where the thumb starts. Feel for each wave of blood as it pushes through the arteries.

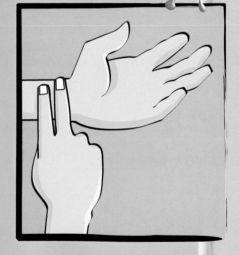

INTERNET LINKS: www.e-learningforkids.org/health/lesson/heart-and-circulation

In the blood

Blood contains a mixture of cells, chemicals, and fluid. Adults have about 10 pt. (5L) of blood. Every drop is pumped around the body through the blood vessels about once every minute, taking food, oxygen, and heat to the tissues.

WHAT IS A PLATELET?
Platelets are tiny cells in the blood that play a very important part in helping blood clots form and stopping bleeding.

▶ A straw-colored fluid called plasma makes up more than 50 percent of your blood. It contains more than 100 important chemicals, including chemical messengers called hormones, nutrients, and antibodies that protect against infection.

plasma

red blood cell

platelet

VOCABULARY

antibodies
Chemicals that help fight infections

bacteria
Tiny organisms that cause infections

hormones
Chemical messengers sent around the body

▶ Blood contains many red blood cells. Their job is to pick up oxygen in the lungs and carry it to the tissues.

white blood cell

HOW YOUR SKIN HEALS

The body has a special system to repair damage to the skin. Cells and fluid leak from the blood vessels to form a thick clot. This seals the area and forms a scab, stopping germs from getting into the wound.

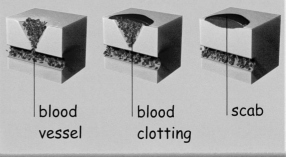

blood vessel

blood clotting

scab

◄ There are far fewer white cells than red cells in the blood. White blood cells protect us from infection by tracking down invading microorganisms, attacking them with chemicals called antibodies, and swallowing them up.

► Many people give some of their blood to be used by others who have lost blood in an accident. Receiving blood in this way is called having a blood transfusion.

Breathing

Every breath you take pulls air into your body. Air contains a gas called oxygen that the cells must have to work properly. It is your breathing system that gets the oxygen to the cells.

▶ The breathing system is made up of a series of tubes, or airways, that carry air from the outside world all the way down into two large, spongy organs in your chest called the lungs.

▶ As air is drawn in through the nose, it is cleaned and moistened. Hairs in your nostrils trap any large particles of dust and dirt, while a layer of sticky mucus collects any smaller particles.

▶ The air then passes down through the voice box (larynx), into the windpipe (trachea), and through breathing tubes (bronchi) into the lungs. The ribs move in and out to control the flow of air.

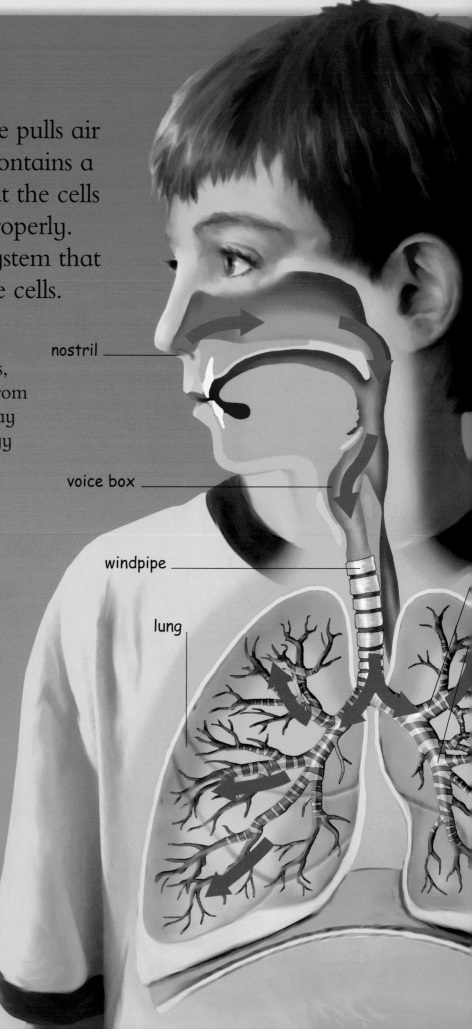

nostril

voice box

windpipe

lung

breathing
tubes

▲ When we breathe out, stale air full of a waste gas called carbon dioxide is pushed out of the body. By squeezing hard with your tummy muscles, you can force air out quickly to blow bubbles or blow out candles.

HOLD YOUR BREATH

In a sport called free diving, a person takes a single breath in and dives as deep as they can. They may go down 525 ft. (160m), which is more than 50 times deeper than a swimming pool.

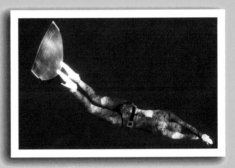

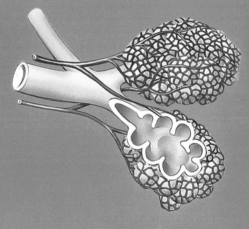

▲ The breathing tubes get smaller until they open up into tiny, bubblelike sacs called alveoli, which look like bunches of grapes. There, oxygen passes into the bloodstream while carbon dioxide moves the other way, out of the bloodstream and into the gas in the alveoli.

WHY DOESN'T FOOD FALL INTO YOUR LUNGS?

As you swallow, a flap of tissue folds down over the top of the windpipe, closing it off and sending food down your gullet instead.

INTERNET LINKS: www.e-learningforkids.org/health/lesson/respiratory-system

When the body goes wrong

Our bodies are very complex machines that we push to the limit all the time. All sorts of things can harm us, from accidents to infections, so it is not surprising that things often go wrong!

▶ Your bones are extremely strong, but if you have a bad accident, they may break. Most broken bones can be set in a plaster cast. This holds the bones together until they are healed by the surrounding tissue.

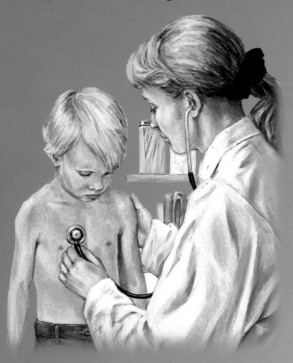

▲ Over the past 100 years, we have discovered so much about how the human body works that there are now treatments for most illnesses. When things do go wrong, doctors and nurses can help us get better.

WHAT CAUSES AN INFECTION?

Infections are caused by many different germs that may be in the air we breathe, the water we drink, the food we eat, or on things we touch.

▲ Sometimes a person needs an operation to remove a diseased part of their body. The surgeons must wash their hands thoroughly and put on gowns, hats, masks, and gloves to prevent spreading bacteria to the patient.

▶ Almost everyone gets an infection, such as a cold, now and then. This virus gives you a fever, sore throat, and a stuffed or runny nose, but most people get better from it very quickly.

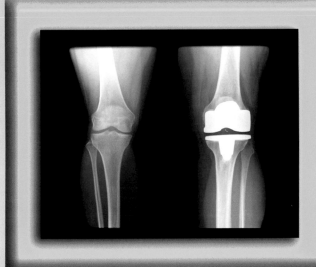

ARTIFICIAL LIMBS

Doctors can now remove many parts of the body and replace them with artificial organs or tissues donated by others. For example, joints such as knees can be replaced and so can organs such as the heart and lungs.

Now you know!

◄ Every human has the same basic shape and body parts, but we all have different builds, coloring, and personalities.

► All our bodies are very similar on the inside, packed with important structures that carry out vital jobs to keep us going.

► We are made from trillions of microscopic cells. Each cell has a nucleus at the center that tells it what to do.

▲ We have skills that no other animals have, allowing us to invent things and change the world to meet our needs.

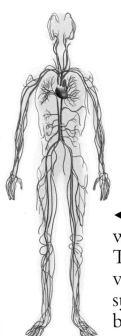

► Cells of the same type work together in tissues. Tissues are grouped together to form organs, such as the liver. Each organ has its own special job to do.

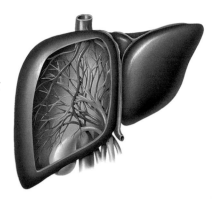

◄ Two or more organs work together in a system. The heart and blood vessels form the circulatory system, which pumps blood around the body.

► The body can go wrong sometimes, making us sick. Doctors and nurses can help make us better again.

Growing and changing

From the moment your life began, your body started to grow and change. At first, you grew and changed a lot very quickly. Now you are still growing, but not quite as fast. Even when you are an adult and you stop growing, your body will continue to change in different ways.

The human life cycle

Life follows the same pattern for every living thing. Humans start as tiny, vulnerable babies, grow and mature into independent adults, and then become old and die. This is the human life cycle.

▶ Most people grow up to have children of their own and start a new generation. Some people have many children, while others have only one or adopt children. Each family is different.

▶ Families follow different patterns. Sometimes several generations, such as parents, children, aunts, uncles, and grandparents, live together. Other families prefer to live more quietly with only parents and their own children together.

AMAZING!
In some parts of the world, people are especially long lived. On the Japanese island of Okinawa, for example, more than 900 people out of a total population of one million are more than 100 years old. Far fewer people in the United States live this long.

CREATIVE CORNER

Who are your relatives?
Draw a family tree. Start at the top with your grandparents and draw lines to show their children (your parents, aunts, and uncles). Then add lines to show their children (you, your brothers, sisters, and any cousins you might have).

▲ Both health and illness can run in families. For example, if your parents are nearsighted, you may be, too. And also, if your grandparents are healthy and long lived, then it is more likely you will be, too!

◀ Many cultures like to celebrate when a person reaches a certain stage in life. This might be when a child becomes an adult or the age at which they can vote, which is 18 or 21 in many countries.

INTERNET LINKS: www.e-learningforkids.org/life-skills/lesson/family

Your genes

Why do we look the way we do, and why do we often look very similar to our parents, brothers, or sisters? The answer is in our genes, a complex recipe or code of instructions that tells our bodies how to make and repair themselves.

chromosome

nucleus

▼ Parents pass their genes on to their children. You carry some of both of your parents' genes, and this is why you may have some of their physical features. You may be able to see a likeness between you and your grandparents, too.

AMAZING!
You have 23 pairs of chromosomes in every cell, or 46 chromosomes in total. One chromosome in each pair comes from your mother, and one comes from your father.

DNA

▶ Each cell in your body contains a copy of your genes. They are made from a chemical called deoxyribonucleic acid (DNA), which has a special "double helix" spiral shape. Genes are stored in stringlike strands called chromosomes in the nucleus, or control center, of each cell.

▲ We all have almost exactly the same genes, so we all have arms, legs, a head, a body, and the same organs inside. A few of our genes are different, however, which is why we have different hair color and body shapes.

▼ As well as inheriting physical features from our parents, we may also inherit some of their personality or talents. Being good at math, music, or sports may depend on our genes . . . but a lot of hard work is involved, too!

▲ One pair of chromosomes, called the X and Y, or sex, chromosomes, decides whether you are a boy or a girl. Girls have two X chromosomes, while boys have one X and one Y chromosome.

INTERNET LINKS: http://kidshealth.org/kid/talk/qa/what_is_gene.html

Making babies

When life begins, special cells from a woman and a man, called an egg and a sperm, join together to form a single new cell inside the woman's womb. That new cell divides and grows until it becomes a baby.

sperm

▶ Each microscopic sperm has an oval head with a nucleus where the genes are stored. It also has a long whiplike tail, which helps it swim through the female reproductive system to find an egg.

head

tail

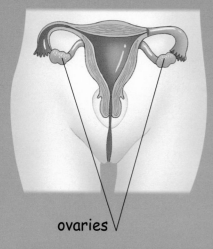

ovaries

testis

▲ A woman's eggs are made in a pair of special organs called the ovaries. One egg is produced each month. The man's sperm is made in a pair of organs called the testes.

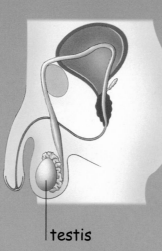

WHAT HAPPENS TO MAKE TWINS?
Fraternal, or nonidentical, twins are formed if two eggs, released at the same time, are separately fertilized. Identical twins are formed when one fertilized egg splits into two.

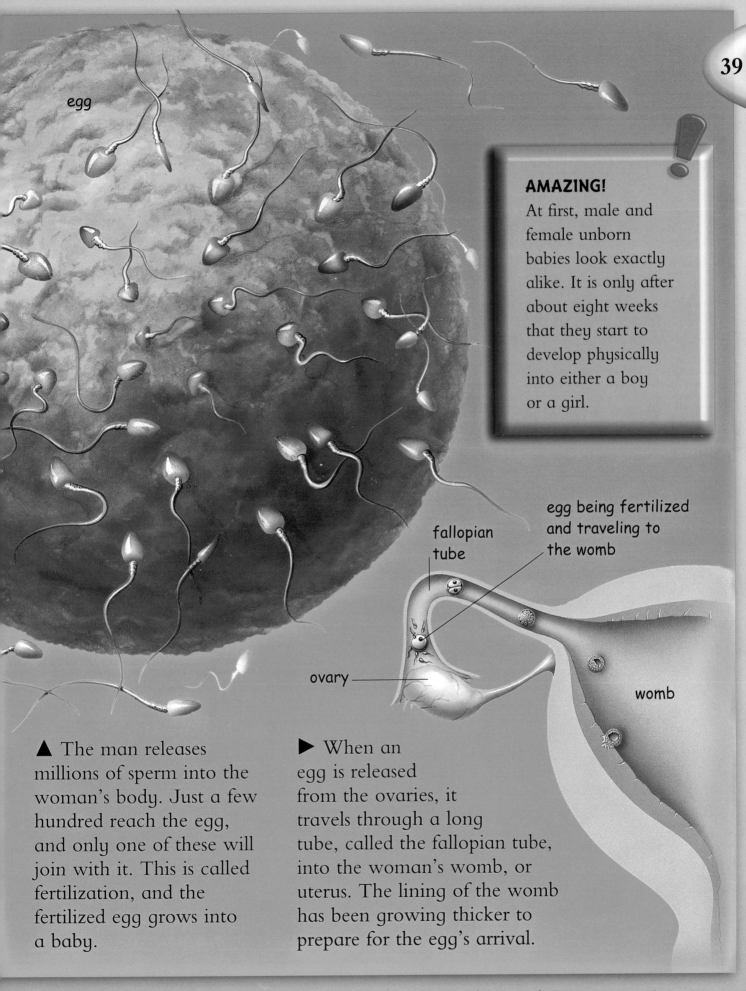

egg

AMAZING!
At first, male and female unborn babies look exactly alike. It is only after about eight weeks that they start to develop physically into either a boy or a girl.

egg being fertilized and traveling to the womb

fallopian tube

ovary

womb

▲ The man releases millions of sperm into the woman's body. Just a few hundred reach the egg, and only one of these will join with it. This is called fertilization, and the fertilized egg grows into a baby.

▶ When an egg is released from the ovaries, it travels through a long tube, called the fallopian tube, into the woman's womb, or uterus. The lining of the womb has been growing thicker to prepare for the egg's arrival.

INTERNET LINKS: www.sciencemuseum.org.uk/WhoAmI/FindOutMore/Yourbody/Wheredidyoucomefrom

Life in the womb

Once the sperm and egg have joined together to form a new life, pregnancy begins. Pregnancy is the time when the baby (now called a fetus) grows and develops inside its mother's womb until it is ready to be born. Pregnancy usually lasts about 38 weeks, or nine months.

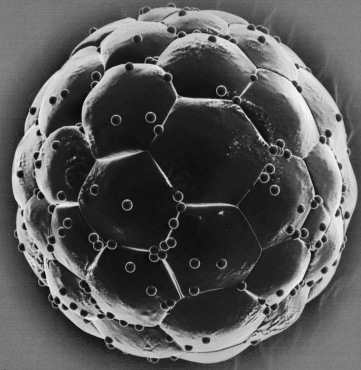

▲ The fertilized egg divides again and again to form a ball of cells. After about a week, this ball of cells settles down into the special lining of the womb.

VOCABULARY

fallopian tube
The tube from the ovary to the womb that the egg travels through

placenta
The organ that connects the fetus (baby) to the inside of the womb

umbilical cord
The cord carrying nutrients to the fetus

womb (or uterus)
The organ in which the fetus develops

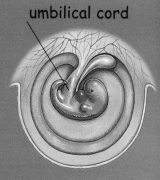
umbilical cord

► Once the ball of cells has implanted, an organ called the placenta forms. This connects the fetus to its mother through blood vessels in the umbilical cord, which supply it with food and oxygen.

placenta

◄ By five weeks of pregnancy, the fetus is still only the size of a pea, but it is changing fast. There are tiny buds that will develop into arms and legs, and the heart has started beating.

MOVING AND KICKING!

At just 12 weeks of pregnancy, the fetus is already moving around, frowning, and opening its eyes inside the womb. From about 16 weeks, it may be possible to feel it kicking.

◀ By 12 weeks, all the muscles, bones, and limbs are formed and the baby is recognizable. The internal organs are still developing, however, and the fetus still has to grow 100 times in weight before it is ready to be born.

▶ During pregnancy, the mother's body changes to help her carry the fetus. Her heart works twice as hard to deliver blood to the womb, and her breasts change as they get ready to produce milk for the newborn baby.

A new baby

When a baby is ready to be born, the mother feels powerful movements, called contractions, in the muscles of her womb. These contractions push the baby out into the world in a process called labor. It may last for many hours.

HOW BIG IS A NEWBORN BABY?
A newborn baby usually weighs about 7.5 lb. (3.5kg) and measures about 20 in. (50cm) from the top of its head to its feet.

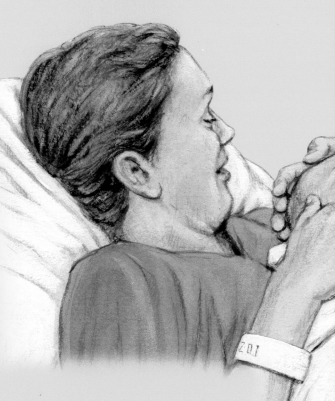

CUTTING THE CORD
Once a baby has been born, the umbilical cord that connected the baby to its mother in the womb and supplied it with food and oxygen can be cut.

▶ A newborn baby cannot move much or feed itself, and it will be years before he or she can survive on his or her own. Breast milk gives the baby all the nutrients that it needs in the early days of its life.

▲ As soon as the baby is born, he or she is checked by a doctor or nurse. Then the baby is wrapped in a warm blanket and given to the mother and father so that they can start to get to know their newborn.

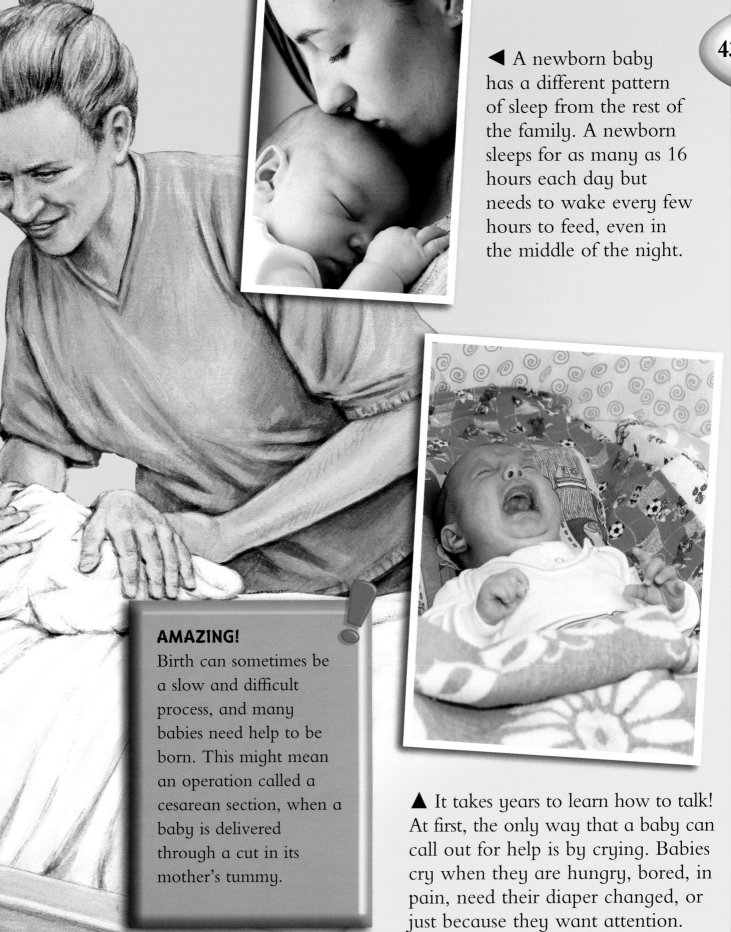

◀ A newborn baby has a different pattern of sleep from the rest of the family. A newborn sleeps for as many as 16 hours each day but needs to wake every few hours to feed, even in the middle of the night.

AMAZING!
Birth can sometimes be a slow and difficult process, and many babies need help to be born. This might mean an operation called a cesarean section, when a baby is delivered through a cut in its mother's tummy.

▲ It takes years to learn how to talk! At first, the only way that a baby can call out for help is by crying. Babies cry when they are hungry, bored, in pain, need their diaper changed, or just because they want attention.

INTERNET LINKS: http://whyzz.com/why-do-babies-sleep-so-much

The first few weeks

A newborn baby is completely helpless, but in the first few weeks and months of life, a lot of changes start to happen. As the baby grows and develops, he or she becomes stronger and more active and begins to learn about the world around him or her.

▶ At first, a baby is very weak and cannot control its own muscles. The neck is floppy, so the head must always be gently supported. Gradually, the baby learns to control its muscles and hold up its own head.

DO BABIES GET COLD?

Small babies cannot control their temperature, so they can easily get too cold or too hot. They should be dressed in several layers of clothes.

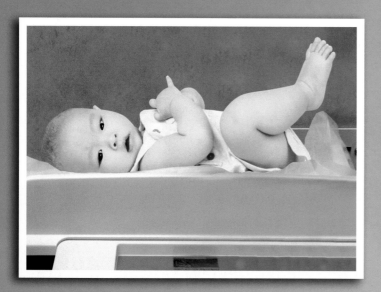

◀ In the first few days, a newborn baby may lose weight, but once the baby starts to feed properly, he or she grows very quickly. A baby's weight may triple in the first year, and he or she will keep on growing after that.

MOTHER'S MILK

A mother produces about 2 pt. (1L) of breast milk each day, which contains the perfect mixture of nutrients for her baby. Some mothers prefer to use a bottle to feed their baby with a special artificial milk called "formula."

◄ Some parts of a child's body grow fast, some more slowly. A baby has a large head compared with its body, giving it a different shape from a toddler. The baby's body, arms, and legs will grow fast and catch up.

AMAZING!

As soon as a baby is born, it starts to learn who its parents and family are. Babies like to stare at faces and listen to the voices of those around them. Soon a strong bond develops between babies and their caregivers.

▲ Babies can see light, shapes, and movement as soon as they are born. They can see far enough to watch their mother's face while they feed or watch a mobile moving above them in their crib.

INTERNET LINKS: http://kidshealth.org/kid/feeling/home_family/new_baby.html

The first two years

Newborn babies learn fast. They start to find out about the world around them very early on. By the age of two, most babies can move themselves around and ask for the things they want.

▼ As babies gain control of their muscles, they learn to roll over, sit up, and crawl. By the age of one, they can usually pull themselves up to stand, which helps strengthen their legs and body. Then they start to walk.

CREATIVE CORNER

Make your own baby diary

Ask your parents for some pictures of you as a baby of different ages. Stick these onto poster board and add some interesting facts, such as your birth weight and stories about your early life.

◀ By about five to six weeks old, babies have probably learned to smile, which is one of the first ways they communicate besides crying. Smiling shows that a baby can see a person's face, make sense of it, and make a smile in return.

AMAZING!
Doctors and nurses weigh and measure babies every few months to check that they are growing as they should. By the age of two, most children have grown to half their adult height and weigh about 26 lb. (12kg).

▶ Babies start talking at about eight weeks old. First they make cooing noises like "aah" and "ooh," and then they start to make simple words such as "mama" or "dog," copying more complex sounds made by the people around them.

WHY DO TINY BABIES GRAB AT THINGS?
Newborn babies curl their hand to grasp if the palm of their hand is stroked. This movement, which they do without thinking, is called a reflex.

▶ By the age of six months, babies can see more clearly and can make a pinching movement with their fingers and thumbs. This allows them to pick up small objects and even start to feed themselves with a spoon.

Exploring everything

By the age of two, a child is very active, exploring their surroundings by opening doors, pulling things out of drawers, pushing, touching, emptying, and tasting. He or she is learning all the skills of being a human.

▶ After learning how to walk, the next goal is learning to run, skip, dance, and catch a ball. At the age of two or three, many toddlers can jump off a step, hop on one foot, ride a tricycle, use crayons, and do a simple jigsaw puzzle.

▶ Playing games with other children is more than just fun. It helps children practice new skills. Most children enjoy playing with others, and as they get older, they learn to share toys or to work together as a team.

◀ As they grow up, children develop a sense of humor and learn to tell jokes and get into mischief. Very young children cannot control their emotions, however, and may quickly change from laughing to having a temper tantrum.

AMAZING!
By the time you are two, you normally know about 50 different words but only use about 40, and many of these may be difficult to understand, especially for strangers. By three, most of your speech is understandable, and by age six you may know more than 13,000 words.

CAN YOU FIND?
1. A girl skipping
2. A boy and a girl running
3. A girl on a jungle gym
4. A boy and a girl playing catch with a ball
5. A boy and a girl arguing

◀ At two years old, a child may put two or three words together, but by the age of three, they are using up to five words to form simple sentences. They may also enjoy singing songs or rhymes.

▲ You probably had all of your baby teeth ("milk teeth"), a full set of 20. These appear by the age of three and last until your larger, adult teeth come in.

Doing things yourself

By the age of four or five, most children start doing more and more things for themselves without the help of their parents. They know how to dress themselves, use the bathroom, and feed themselves and want to learn to do many other things, too.

▶ Children at this age love finding out how to make things, such as baking a cake or building a fort. They have a lot of questions about the world and enjoy listening to people telling them the answers or explaining how things work.

AMAZING!
Some children start to play a musical instrument when they are just five years old. The famous Austrian composer Wolfgang Amadeus Mozart wrote his first musical pieces at the age of five, by which time he could already play the piano and the violin.

▲ They know the sounds of many words and have probably started to learn how to write them down and read them, too. The first step is learning the alphabet.

◀ A four-year-old may like to feel more independent and is not upset if mom or dad leaves him or her with other people for a little while. It is fun to have friends and other children around to play with.

▲ At this age, children usually do as they are asked and understand what is right and what is wrong. They know that they should take turns and share, but sometimes they still fight over toys or have a tantrum.

IT'S ALL MAKE-BELIEVE

Children often love to play make-believe games and hear fairy tales, but it may be difficult to figure out what is pretend and what is real. They may be scared of the dark or of imaginary monsters.

Now you are six

At six years old, you can stand up for yourself and take control of your world. You can do all sorts of exciting things, such as playing sports, painting pictures, reading books, and learning to play a musical instrument.

▶ Now that you are about six or seven, you are learning to understand other people's feelings better. There are many new friends to get to know and have fun with, including special "best friends," and you are discovering what makes all of you happy and sad.

2 years   4 years   6-7 years   10 years

▲ At around six to seven, your legs are growing faster than any other parts of your body! This makes you taller and more of an adult shape than a shorter-legged toddler.

HOW IS MY BODY CHANGING?

In the first ten years of life, your weight will increase to about 75 lb. (35kg)—about ten times your baby weight. You will be almost three times taller, too, at about 4 ft. 7 in. (140cm).

► You are strong, full of energy, and able to follow instructions. You can also concentrate for longer periods and are ready to try different things. Many sports clubs are open to you at this age, so you can discover what you like to do.

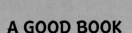

► You will have a gap-toothed smile for a while! Most children start to lose their baby teeth (also called milk teeth) at age six. One by one, the teeth become loose and fall out painlessly to make room for new, permanent adult teeth.

A GOOD BOOK

By the age of seven, you can probably read quite well, and you might like to snuggle up with a book at the end of the day. It is a very good way to get to sleep at night.

INTERNET LINKS: http://whyzz.com/why-do-we-grow

Boys and puberty

Between the ages of about 12 and 18, your body will start to change again. This is a time of rapid growth and development known as puberty, and the changes it brings will make you ready for adult life.

AMAZING!
By the time he is 15, a boy's head will have grown to its full adult size of about a seventh the length of his body.

▶ Puberty usually begins around age 12–14 in boys. Changes that occur in their bodies over the next few years prepare them for adulthood and for reproduction, allowing them to have children of their own one day.

▶ During puberty, boys may suddenly grow as much as 4 in. (10cm) in a year. This is known as a growth spurt, and it usually happens around age 14. Their shoulders become broader and their bodies more muscular.

WHY DOES A BOY'S VOICE GET DEEPER AT PUBERTY?
The larynx (voice box) grows, forming a lump in the neck called the Adam's apple and making a boy's voice deeper.

VOCABULARY

acne
The pimples that many teenagers get

adolescence
The time from the start of puberty to adulthood

puberty
The process of physical change from child to adult

testes
The small organs that hang outside a boy's body and produce sperm

WHAT CHANGES OCCUR DURING PUBERTY?

The testes get larger and begin to produce sperm. The penis also grows, and hair starts to appear around it and on the chest, armpits, and face.

▲ Boys (and girls) often become more moody during puberty as they start to think more about who they are and where their futures lie. Suddenly life does not seem so carefree anymore.

▲ It may be difficult to get used to the changes of puberty. Just when boys start to think more about how they look and how they can find a girlfriend, their bodies sweat more, they may have pimples, or acne, on their skin, and facial hair begins to grow.

Girls and puberty

Girls also go through puberty as their bodies get ready for adulthood, but these changes usually start a little earlier than for boys, at about 10–12 years of age. The first visible sign is that the breasts start to grow and the nipples get larger.

WHAT STARTS PUBERTY?
Many factors work together to trigger the start of puberty, but one of the most important is when the body reaches a certain size and weight.

► Deep inside the pelvis, the two ovaries start to produce an egg each month, as the body prepares to have a baby one day. Until then, the special lining of the womb breaks down each month and is released through the vagina as blood. This is known as menstruation, or a period.

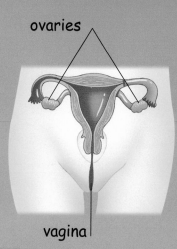

ovaries

vagina

ACNE
Most teenagers have to cope with pimples called acne on their faces from time to time. It has nothing to do with eating fatty foods or not washing properly. It is simply caused by the changes of puberty!

ADULTHOOD

Many cultures have rituals or ceremonies to mark adulthood. When Jewish girls reach 12 years old and Jewish boys reach 13 years old, they pass through the ceremony of bat or bar mitzvah.

◀ Like boys, girls may find puberty difficult. They have to get used to changes in their bodies, their feelings, and their relationships. They have monthly periods to get used to as well.

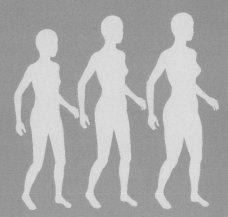

9 years   12 years   18 years

MOODS

Many girls find that they feel a little sad, tired, and irritable for a day or two before each monthly period.

▲ A girl's growth spurt usually occurs around the age of 12. She becomes more curvy in shape as her hips widen. Hair also starts to grow in her armpits and around her vagina.

Grown up at last!

Once puberty is complete, you will have reached your full adult height. You will not become any taller, but you will continue to develop in other ways as you study for school, build a career, and decide what you want to do with your life.

▼ Some physical changes continue in early adulthood. Young men may become more muscular, and the brain is still developing for both men and women. Reading, learning, and trying new things help form new connections between the nerve cells and develop intelligence.

WHEN DO WE BECOME ADULTS?
We become adults once we have gone through all the changes of puberty, usually around the ages of 16–18.

HOW YOU HAVE GROWN

At 18, you will be about twice as tall as when you were two but will weigh five times as much. You will have grown up and out!

▲ Most adults settle down with a partner and think about having children, but every family is different. Some people have many children, while others choose not to have any.

◄ Most people need to work throughout their adult lives to earn enough money to take care of themselves and their families. From office work to more physical jobs, there are thousands of different jobs to choose from.

AMAZING!

The age at which a person is recognized as an adult by law varies from country to country. It may be as early as 16 or as late as 21.

INTERNET LINKS: http://whyzz.com/why-dont-adults-have-to-go-to-school

Adulthood

People have to work hard to take care of their bodies and keep them in the best condition. A lot can go wrong, and although we stop growing, our bodies are always changing and repairing themselves.

AMASING!
Some parts of the body can regrow completely. If you scrape off some skin, it will grow back again within days. The liver can also regenerate itself even if three-fourths of it has been removed.

◀ Many of the body's cells divide and grow throughout our lives. Nails and skin are worn away or damaged, and every day we lose hairs that need to be replaced.

HOW DOES THE HEART CHANGE?
A young adult's heart beats up to 200 times a minute if he or she runs fast. By age 80, it will go no faster than about 145 beats a minute.

▶ With every year that passes, our bodies burn less fuel for energy. Adults rush around much less than children do. If we continue to eat the same amount as we used to, we may get fatter. Adults need a lot of exercise, just like children!

▲ From about age 40 onward, our eyes start to change, and it becomes more difficult to read or see details. By 55, most people wear glasses some of the time. Our eyes also become drier, as we make fewer tears.

▲ Most older adults have to fight at least one type of disease that stops the body from working well. Arthritis, for example, can affect the finger joints and make playing a musical instrument or simply holding something difficult.

INTERNET LINKS: http://kidshealth.org/kid/grownup/index.html#cat20183

Aging

As we get older, our tissues and organs gradually stop working as well as they used to. The body becomes less able to repair itself, and diseases become more common. Some people age more quickly than others.

AMAZING!
There are good things about growing older, too! Age brings wisdom, patience, and experience, which help us deal with the difficult things in life. Some people climb mountains or run marathons in later life, and some leaders lead their countries in old age.

► Some parts of the body start to age almost as soon as we reach adulthood, and it is not long before it shows. Many men, for example, start to go bald in their 20s or 30s.

◄ The most obvious signs of aging can be seen in the skin and hair. The skin becomes less elastic and fine creases called wrinkles appear, especially around the eyes and mouth. The hair loses its color and begins to look gray or white.

◀ Hobbies such as reading and doing puzzles help our minds stay sharp. It is also important to exercise to keep the muscles and bones strong. This is because our muscles become weaker and we lose our sense of balance as we get older.

▶ When people become very old, they often need help from their families to do even simple things such as bathing, getting dressed, and preparing food. The final stage in the human life cycle is death. We live much longer now than people used to, but we will all die one day.

DEATH CEREMONIES

Special ceremonies or rituals are often held to mark a person's death. In many Christian cultures, people wear black clothes at a funeral as a sign of respect, but at a Hindu cremation, it is traditional for friends and family to wear white.

INTERNET LINKS: http://whyzz.com/why-do-people-have-wrinkles

Now you know!

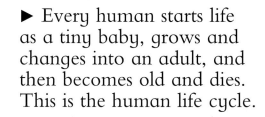

▶ Every human starts life as a tiny baby, grows and changes into an adult, and then becomes old and dies. This is the human life cycle.

◀ Inside the nucleus of each cell is a code called DNA, which controls how the body grows and develops throughout life.

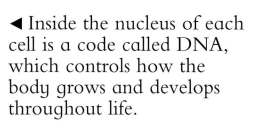

◀ A new life begins when a sperm from a man fertilizes an egg from a woman.

▶ A baby grows inside its mother's womb for about 38 weeks. Then it is ready to be born.

▶ Babies are born helpless, but they soon grow into more independent children.

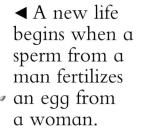

▼ As people grow older, they have to work hard to take care of their bodies. Adults need to do a lot of exercise, too!

Food and digestion

Our bodies need a constant supply of food and liquids to keep going and stay healthy. We need what is called a balanced diet—the right mixture of many different types of foods. The digestive system is designed to break down those foods and supply all the cells of the body with the nutrients they need.

Food for life

We need food to survive, but it is much more than simply fuel for our bodies. Eating gives us pleasure, and when we are cold or tired, food can be warm and comforting. Food brings families and friends together and is part of many of our celebrations.

◀ Early humans were hunter-gatherers who lived on vegetables, nuts, and berries. If they were near water, they could catch fish. Meat was a rare treat. After developing cooking skills, they could eat beans, potatoes, and grains (from wheat, rice, oats, barley, and corn). This sort of diet provided all the nutrients that people needed.

◀ Nowadays we eat a lot of processed and packaged foods that may not be good for us. Many of these foods contain more sugar, salt, and fat than we need and not enough of other important nutrients.

CREATIVE CORNER

Make a food diary

Make a food diary to record what you eat each week. There should be a mixture of different foods, including meat or dairy foods, fresh vegetables and fruit, and some starchy or cereal foods such as potatoes, rice, pasta, or bread. Find out if you eat a healthy, balanced diet.

▶ Sharing a meal is a great way for families and friends to come together. People often celebrate with special foods, such as roast turkey at Christmas or Thanksgiving.

What we eat

Travel around the globe and you will find thousands of different foods, recipes, and meals. Some cheap foods, including rice, potatoes, and cereals such as wheat, form the basis of most people's diets around the world. Think how often you eat rice, pasta, bread, or potatoes. Other people are doing it, too!

AMAZING!
It has been estimated that by the age of 70 you will have eaten your way through the contents of a large grocery store and consumed more than 53 million calories.

▲ Your idea of a normal breakfast may be very different from someone living in another country. There are many different ways to combine basic foods such as vegetables, meat, and fruit and cook them to make a meal.

▲ Until recent times, people made their meals fresh every day from basic ingredients such as vegetables, meat, cheese, and grains. These sorts of meals usually contain a good balance of the nutrients we need, including vitamins and minerals.

CAN YOU FIND?
1. A bowl of fruit
2. A plate of salad
3. A pizza
4. A cake
5. Green beans
6. Fried eggs
7. A piece of toast

RELIGIOUS DIETS
Some people follow a special diet for religious reasons. Jewish people, for example, eat a flat bread called matzo instead of normal bread during the religious holiday of Passover.

▲ Many people, especially in Western countries, now eat a lot of food that has been made in factories. These processed, packaged foods, such as pizzas and cakes, may be quick and easy to prepare, but it is not good to have too many of them because they do not provide a balanced diet.

▲ People who avoid eating any meat are called vegetarians. They often believe that this sort of diet is kinder to animals or the environment or that it is simply healthier for them.

Choosing healthy foods

We all need a mixture of different foods to stay healthy. If you were to eat one type of food, such as a cheese sandwich or chicken nuggets, for every meal, you would get enough energy to survive but not enough of all the different nutrients you need. You would be very bored, too!

▶ Your body needs a lot of a nutrient called protein to build new cells, grow, and repair itself. There is protein in foods from animal sources such as meat, fish, eggs, and dairy foods and in cereals, soy products, nuts, beans, and legumes.

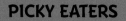

PICKY EATERS

Some animals are able to live on one or two foods alone. Koala bears eat only eucalyptus leaves, giant pandas feed on bamboo, and anteaters live on ants and termites.

▼ Foods rich in carbohydrates are sometimes called "go" foods because they give you energy. You should eat plenty of them, but remember to exercise, too. They include bread, rice, potatoes, pasta, cereals, fruit, root vegetables, and dairy products.

AMAZING!
Your weight depends on how much energy (or calories) you eat and how much you burn when you exercise. If you ate an extra four regular candy bars a day without getting more exercise, you would gain 2 lb. (1kg) in weight each week.

CREATIVE CORNER

Take a look at food labels
Many labels show the amounts of protein, carbohydrate, fat, and energy the foods contain. Find some foods that are good for growing (protein) and "going" (carbohydrates).

▲ Nutrients called vitamins and minerals help keep the body in tiptop condition. We get vitamins and minerals from all sorts of foods but especially from fresh fruit and vegetables. You can never eat too many of these healthy foods!

Fats and fiber

As well as protein, carbohydrates, vitamins, and minerals, we also need many other types of nutrients to do important jobs in our bodies. These nutrients include fats and fiber. A balanced diet should give us plenty of these, too.

ARE RAW VEGETABLES GOOD FOR YOU?

Raw vegetables are usually better for you than cooked ones (although beans and potatoes must be cooked). Try to include plenty of raw vegetables in your diet.

◀ You may think that fat is bad for you, but we all need some for growth and repair and to give us energy. Types of fats include butter; oils from vegetables, nuts, and fish; and animal fat on meat.

▶ Fiber is important because it helps all the food move smoothly through your digestive system and stops the system from getting blocked up. There is a lot of fiber in cereals, beans, lentils, fruit, and vegetables.

AMADING!

Fat provides a lot of calories. Polar explorers eat a lot of fat so that they have enough energy to burn to keep warm in the freezing conditions. Most of us need only small amounts of healthy fats from vegetable or fish oil.

▲ Most foods contain a mixture of nutrients. Whole-wheat bread contains carbohydrates and fiber from the grains that the bread flour is made of. Spread butter or mayonnaise on it and you will get some fat. Then add a slice of cheese or ham and get some protein, too!

WHAT'S IN THE SKIN?

The skins of many fruits and vegetables are packed full of fiber and vitamins. So when you are eating apples, pears, plums, or potatoes, for example, try to eat the skin or the peel if you can. It's important to wash fruit and vegetables in clean water before eating them.

INTERNET LINKS: http://kidshealth.org/kid/stay_healthy/food/fat.html

Vitamins and minerals

As well as protein and carbohydrates, our bodies need a constant supply of additional nutrients and chemicals known as vitamins and minerals to stay healthy.

AMAZING!

Thousands of years ago, ancient Egyptians knew that people who could not see well at night might see better if they ate liver. Nowadays we know that this condition, called night blindness, is caused by a lack of vitamin A. Liver is full of this vitamin, which is why it helped.

▼ Vitamin D helps make our bones, muscles, and the immune system strong. We get some from foods such as oily fish, but most of it comes from the effect of sunlight on our skin. A little sunshine each day is good for us.

▲ We need vitamins A, C, D, E, K, and eight types of vitamin B! They do a lot of jobs in the body. All those B vitamins keep the nervous system healthy, while vitamin C, in citrus fruit such as oranges, helps wounds heal and keeps the immune system healthy.

▶ Seven minerals are especially important—calcium, chlorine, magnesium, phosphorous, potassium, sodium, and sulfur—but we also need smaller amounts of many others. Calcium is good for healthy bones and teeth. We get it from milk and other dairy foods, soybeans, and dark green, leafy vegetables such as broccoli.

WHICH FOODS CONTAIN A LOT OF VITAMIN C?

All of these foods contain a lot of vitamin C:
1. Sweet potatoes
2. Red peppers
3. Kiwifruit
4. Strawberries
5. Broccoli

▼ We need the mineral iron for healthy blood and to fight infections. We can get iron from meat, fish, eggs, and dark green, leafy vegetables.

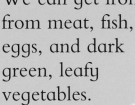

DISEASE AT SEA

Around 250 years ago, sailors on long voyages often suffered from a deadly disease called scurvy, which caused loose teeth and bleeding gums. Naval surgeon Dr. James Lind discovered that eating plenty of fresh citrus fruit, such as limes, prevented scurvy. Later it was proved that it was the vitamin C in the fruit that cured the sailors.

Liquids

As well as eating food, you need to drink plenty of liquids to keep your body working. More than 60 percent of your body weight is made up of water, but you lose it all the time through sweat, urine, and in the moist air you breathe out.

HOW MUCH LIQUID SHOULD I DRINK EACH DAY?
It depends how big you are. The average seven-year-old needs about 1.5 qt. (1.5L), or 6–8 glasses, of water a day. In very hot weather, you need more.

◀ Most foods contain quite a lot of water, and this can give you about one-third of the liquid you need every day. The rest must come from drinks. Plain, normal water is the healthiest way to replenish the liquid levels in your body.

▲ Drinks made from milk are another good way to take in liquid, and they also provide nutrients you need, such as calcium and other minerals. You can also drink fruit juices to keep your water levels up.

▶ Many people like to drink sodas, but these are not always the healthiest choice. They often contain a lot of sugar and can damage the surface of your teeth. You can see what carbonated drinks do to hard substances by leaving a coin in a leftover glass of soda overnight!

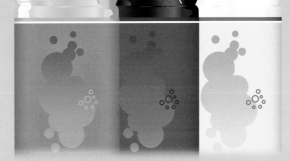

AMAZING!
You can tell if you are drinking enough by looking at your urine. If you make a lot of straw-colored urine that does not smell, you are probably drinking enough. If your urine is very dark, however, you need to drink more.

◀ If you do not drink enough, your body may dry out. This is called dehydration, and it makes you feel sick. This can happen after you have been very active because you get hot and sweat more. Drinking extra liquid beforehand helps.

INTERNET LINKS: http://kidshealth.org/kid/stay_healthy/food/water.html

Into the mouth

Your digestive system is a food factory production line that takes your food and breaks it down into tiny pieces called nutrients. These nutrients pass into the body and are rebuilt into new cells and tissues or burned as fuel. It all starts in your mouth.

▶ The digestive system is made up of a long tube, from the mouth at the top to the anus at the bottom. Food travels through this tube, slowly changing into a slushy soup that is taken into the bloodstream. The pieces you cannot digest are pushed out of the anus as waste.

TEETH

Your teeth are a very important part of the digestive system, and you need to take care of them. Brushing twice a day with a fluoride toothpaste helps keep them clean and strong and able to chew your food.

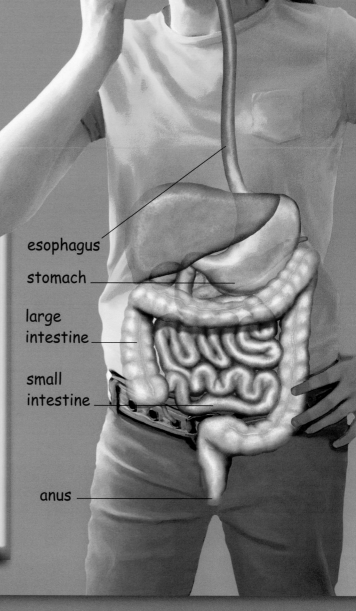

mouth

esophagus

stomach

large intestine

small intestine

anus

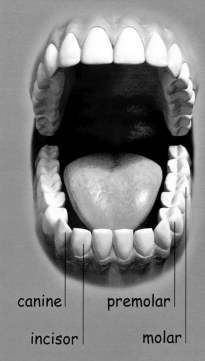

canine

premolar

incisor

molar

◄ Digestion starts when your teeth break food into smaller lumps that you can easily swallow. Sharp incisors at the front cut the food like a knife, pointed canines grip and tear it, while the flat premolars and molars at the back grind it up.

AMAZING!
Your teeth are covered in the hardest substance in the body, which is called enamel. Although it is tough, enamel can easily be damaged by sodas, so try not to drink too many!

► The tongue also helps with chewing and moving food around the mouth. It is a large muscle, mostly hidden behind the jawbone. In fact, if you stick out your tongue, you still see only the tip of it! It is covered in microscopic taste sensors that detect chemical molecules in different foods.

◄ The texture of food, or how it feels when we put it in our mouths, can be almost as important as taste and smell in helping us decide whether we like it. Many people like the texture of chocolate, and some think mushrooms feel slimy.

INTERNET LINKS: http://kidshealth.org/PageManager.jsp?lic=1&article_set=54051&cat_id=20607

Down it goes!

Swallowing is a complex process. Muscles in the mouth, tongue, and throat send the food in the right direction, down into the stomach. The food must be soft and broken up into small pieces, not hard and lumpy, if it is to be swallowed easily.

► Food is easier to chew and swallow when it is wet. Your mouth produces a special liquid called saliva, or spit, that wets it. Saliva also contains chemicals that help start breaking the food down for its nutrients.

VOCABULARY

epiglottis
Flap of tissue that covers the top of the windpipe

esophagus
Tube that carries food down from the mouth into the stomach

saliva
Also called spit, this liquid wets food and starts digestion

AMAZING!

Even the thought or smell of food can be enough to start your body releasing saliva into the mouth. This is why we might call the smell of a delicious cake cooking in the oven "mouth-watering"!

LIP SERVICE

The lips also play a part in swallowing. When we swallow, strong muscles close the lips, helping them seal the mouth and stop food from falling out.

◀ The tongue pushes a lump of food to the back of the mouth. Then it passes down the esophagus. Muscles in the esophagus squeeze, or contract, behind the food, pushing it down toward the stomach.

food

esophagus

WHAT IS THAT THING HANGING DOWN AT THE BACK OF YOUR THROAT?

This is called the uvula, and it makes a lot of watery saliva to keep the throat moist. It also helps in speech.

▲ As food is swallowed, a flap of tissue called the epiglottis folds down to close off the windpipe and stop food from going into the lungs. If food does go into the breathing system, it will make you cough until it is removed.

The stomach

It takes only ten seconds for food to travel down the gullet into the stomach. This large, muscly bag can stretch to up to 20 times its size to hold a full meal. When it has done its work, it slowly, steadily releases the food into the intestines.

▶ The stomach breaks down the chewed-up food to form a thick, creamy liquid. Layers of powerful muscles in the stomach walls squeeze and churn the food again and again, mixing it with digestive juices released from the stomach lining.

▶ After leaving the stomach, the food spends one to two days passing slowly through the intestines. During this time, it is broken down into small molecules of nutrients that can pass through the walls of the intestines into the bloodstream.

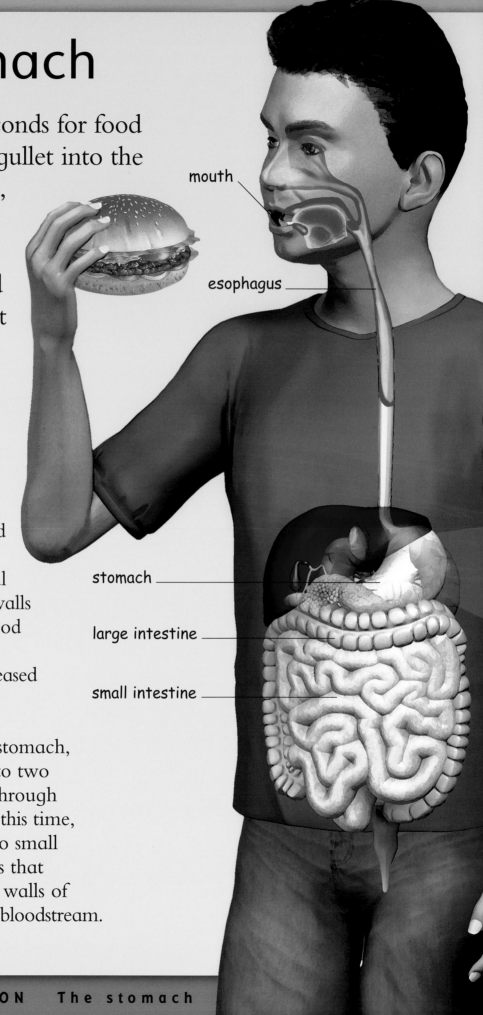

mouth

esophagus

stomach

large intestine

small intestine

WHAT KEEPS FOOD IN THE STOMACH?

The entrance and exit of the stomach are made from powerful muscles, called sphincters, that can close tight or relax to let food through.

AMAZING!

About 2 gal. (7L) of digestive juices are released into the digestive system each day. This includes 3 pt. (1.5L) of saliva, 4 pt. (2L) of stomach juices, 3 pt. (1.5L) of juice from the pancreas, 3 pt. (1.5L) of small intestinal juices, and 1 pt. (0.5L) of bile!

layer of mucus

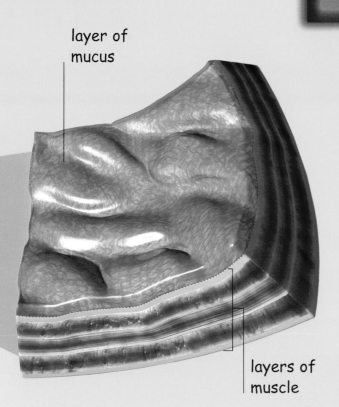

layers of muscle

MANY STOMACHS

Some animals, such as cows, have several compartments in their stomachs. Their food, such as grass, is difficult to digest, so they swallow the food quickly and then bring it back up later, chewing it more thoroughly a second time.

▲ Digestive juices in the stomach contain a very strong chemical called hydrochloric acid. This is powerful enough to digest meat and even small pieces of bone, but it does not harm the stomach itself, which is lined with a layer of protective, jellylike mucus.

INTERNET LINKS: http://kidshealth.org/kid/closet/movies/DSmovie.html?tracking=59983_H#cat119

The intestines

Once food has been broken into tiny particles by the stomach, it travels to the small intestine. In this soft, winding tube, the nutrients in the food pass through the walls of the intestine and into the bloodstream. This is called absorption.

▶ First the food travels into the small intestine. This is a 20-ft. (6-m)-long tube, coiled up below the stomach and liver. It is lined with millions of tiny fingerlike things called villi. These give the intestine a huge folded surface where almost all the important nutrients can be collected.

▶ Then the remaining food particles leave the small intestine and enter the large intestine. Food takes up to 10–12 hours to pass through the large intestine.

DO WE NEED AN APPENDIX?

The appendix is a small tube that is closed at one end. It is joined to the intestines. If it becomes diseased, it can be removed and we can live without it.

liver

large intestine

small intestine

appendix

villi

AMATING!

AMAZING!

If you were to spread the villi that line the small intestine out flat, they would cover an area about the size of a tennis court.

stomach

rectum

anus

FRIENDLY BACTERIA

Billions of bacteria live in the large intestine, but they are not harmful. Instead, these "friendly" bacteria do some essential jobs, including helping defend us from invading germs. We get some of these bacteria from our food, especially raw vegetables and special yogurts.

◀ By the time liquid food reaches the large intestine, most useful nutrients have been removed. The large intestine then absorbs most of the remaining water, leaving waste material and bacteria to be pushed out through the rectum as feces (poop).

▶ Sometimes you can feel your intestines squeezing and moving your food, but more often, you can hear them at work. Listen to your belly or put your ear close to a friend's and you might hear the gurgle of liquid and air bubbles inside.

Digestion factories

Several organs play an essential part in helping the intestines digest your food. These include the liver, the pancreas, and the gallbladder, high up in the abdomen around the stomach and the first part of the small intestine.

▶ Once the blood has collected nutrients from the small intestine, it passes them to the liver. The liver carries out more than 500 different chemical processes, including making special proteins to build new cells, storing sugars and fats, and removing poisons from the blood.

CAN YOU LIVE WITHOUT A LIVER OR A PANCREAS?
No. Scientists are trying to make artificial livers and pancreases, but they have not yet succeeded.

AMAZING!
The liver is one of the few organs in the body that can repair itself and regrow. It can do this even when as much as three-fourths of its cells have been lost or damaged.

gallbladder

small intestine

▼ The liver also makes a substance called bile. This yucky, green liquid is stored in a small bag called the gallbladder and is released into the intestine when you eat. Bile turns food fat into tiny droplets that are easier to digest and absorb.

▼ The pancreas has another important job, producing chemical signals, or hormones, such as insulin, which controls sugar levels in the blood. Some people do not make enough insulin themselves and have an illness called diabetes. They may need to inject themselves with insulin every day.

liver

stomach

pancreas

◀ The pancreas is a tail-shaped organ that empties a complex mixture of digestive juices into the small intestine. These juices help break down carbohydrates, fats, and proteins into microscopic nutrients.

JAUNDICE
A newborn baby's liver often takes a few days to start working properly. Until then, the colored chemicals in bile can build up in the blood and turn the skin yellow. This is called jaundice.

Busy kidneys

Your body gets rid of waste products and poisons by making a liquid waste called urine (you may call it pee or wee). Your kidneys, bladder, and the tubes that drain urine from your body are known as the urinary system.

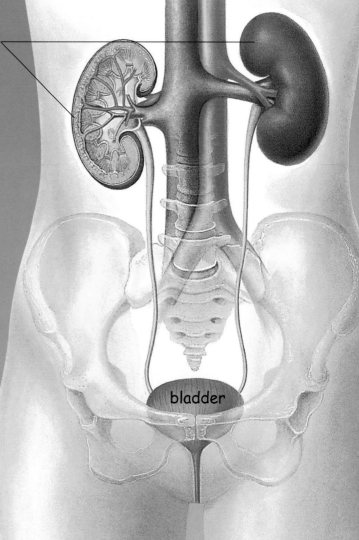

kidneys

bladder

▲ The kidneys work hard to keep just the right amount of water in the body. Every day, you make about 2–4 pt. (1–2L) of urine. The kidneys make less urine if you exercise a lot and lose fluid in sweat or more urine if you drink a lot.

▶ The kidneys are a pair of large bean-shaped organs found at the back of the abdomen. They filter and clean the blood, producing watery urine, which also contains a small amount of salts and other waste chemicals.

WHAT IS A KIDNEY TRANSPLANT?

Every year, thousands of people with a diseased kidney receive one from someone else to replace it. This is called a kidney transplant and can save a life.

◀ Urine trickles from each kidney down tubes into a stretchy, muscular bag called the bladder. It is held there until you are ready to visit the bathroom, when the sphincter muscles in the bladder open and let the urine flow out.

▲ The kidneys also make chemical signals, or hormones. One controls how many new red blood cells are made by marrow in the middle of our bones. Another helps control blood pressure, or how hard blood is pumped around the body.

ARTIFICIAL KIDNEY

We need our kidneys to stay alive, but scientists can now help people with kidney disease. A dialysis machine is like an artificial kidney and can do the work of the kidneys for them.

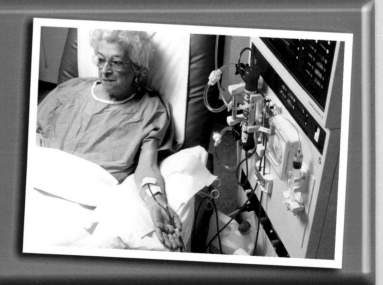

INTERNET LINKS: http://kidshealth.org/PageManager.jsp?lic=1&article_set=54037&cat_id=20607

Throwing out the garbage

Every day, the body produces a lot of waste products, including unwanted chemicals made by the organs, pieces of food that cannot be digested, dead cells that cannot be recycled, and millions of the friendly bacteria that normally live in the bowel. These must all be removed by a process called excretion.

HOW BIG IS YOUR BLADDER?

The bladder is as small as a golf ball when empty but can stretch to hold up to 20 fl. oz. (600mL) of urine before you feel desperate to go to the bathroom.

▶ Once food has traveled through the intestines, the food waste arrives in the last part of the digestive system, called the rectum. This stretchy tube expands to hold food waste inside until you are able to visit the bathroom. Then it is pushed out through an opening called the anus.

AMAZING!

Passing wind, or farting, is perfectly normal and allows the body to get rid of gas that builds up inside the intestines. Everyone passes wind, and the average person may do it up to 25 times a day, although they may be unaware of it.

AMAZING!

Fibrous foods make your feces large and soft, which is good for the gut. People who eat a lot of root vegetables and therefore have a high-fiber diet can pass up to three times more poop than people who have a low-fiber diet.

▲ It is very important to wash your hands after using the bathroom to make sure they are clean. This is because waste matter from the digestive system, which is called feces (or poop), is full of germs.

URINE

Urine is a yellowy-orange fluid made mostly of water but also a lot of salty chemicals such as sodium, potassium, and chloride. These would be harmful if allowed to build up in the body, so the kidneys get rid of them for us.

▲ The body also loses water and salt in sweat and in the air we breathe out. Millions of tiny glands in the skin release sweat liquid onto the surface of the body. Sweat cools you down when you get too hot.

Eating healthily

The food we eat has changed in the past 100 years. We are eating more processed foods instead of meals made from fresh ingredients. We often eat on the run, too, grazing on snacks instead of sitting down with our families. This may not be the most healthy way to eat.

AMAZING!
Some children are allergic to certain foods. If they eat foods such as nuts, eggs, or shellfish, they may have a bad reaction. Others have problems digesting milk and dairy foods.

▶ Sitting down to eat with other people is good for you and can be fun. You can share your news and talk about interesting things. Families should eat together as often as possible, ideally with the television off, too!

▶ It is a good idea to start the day with breakfast. You will work better at school if you have eaten than if you go on an empty stomach. Breakfasts such as cereals, whole-wheat toast, and eggs are especially good because they give you fuel that lasts for hours.

◀ You may feel hungry at bedtime, but a large meal at this time can stop you from sleeping and cause indigestion. The right kinds of foods, such as warm milk and crackers, may help you sleep.

IS FRUIT JUICE GOOD FOR YOU?

Fruit juice is often full of sugar and may be just as unhealthy as a soda. It is better to eat whole fresh fruit.

◀ Learning how to cook is fun! You could try making a tasty sandwich or pizza. Not only do you get to make the kinds of foods that you like, but it is also a great way to discover what foods are healthy.

EATING AND SWIMMING

After a big meal, your body is busy trying to digest the food. If you go swimming immediately afterward, you may suffer indigestion or, more worryingly, painful stomach cramps. It is better to wait at least half an hour before you swim or do other exercise.

Medicines, drugs, and poisons

Sometimes we take certain foods or chemicals because they have special effects on the body that may help keep us healthy or treat an illness. These are called medicines or drugs.

▶ Doctors have developed medicines for many different diseases. Your parents probably keep some at home, such as cough syrup. You may need to use medicines yourself, such as an inhaler if you have asthma.

▼ Medicines should always be used very carefully, according to the instructions, because they can be harmful if used incorrectly or if you take too much. They should be stored safely in a locked cabinet out of reach of children.

ALCOHOLIC DRINKS

Many adults enjoy drinking alcohol, such as beer and wine. However, alcohol is poisonous to the body and should only be drunk in small amounts. A little does no harm, but too much can cause serious health problems.

▶ Some plants and foods are known to have helpful effects on the body. Many people drink camomile tea, for example, because it may help them relax and sleep. Peppermint tea helps the digestive system work well.

CAN PLANTS BE POISONOUS?

Some plants that you can find in your yard are poisonous. Never pick or eat any plants or mushrooms without checking with an adult first.

HEALTH FOODS?

Many foods that you eat today were used years ago as treatments for health problems. Corn flakes, for example, were given to calm down hospital patients, but now we know that cereals are a good basic food for everyone.

◀ Never touch or open bottles of chemicals such as cleaning fluids. Some are poisonous and can make you very sick. Learn to recognize warning labels on the bottles. A skull and crossbones symbol, for example, shows that the bottle contains poison.

INTERNET LINKS: www.drpbody.com/poisons.html

Now you know!

◄ We need to eat several different types of food every day to stay healthy. This is called a balanced diet.

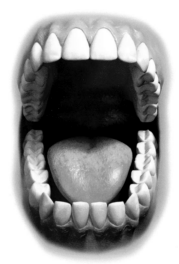

▲ People's diets vary around the world. Your meals may be very different compared to someone in a different country.

◄ Food travels through the digestive system, which breaks it down into tiny pieces.

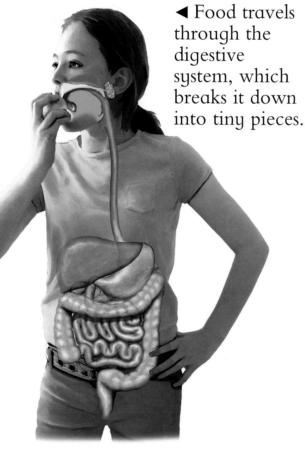

▲ Digestion starts in the mouth. Food is moistened by saliva and crushed by the teeth before being swallowed.

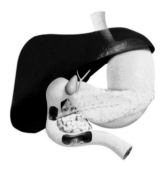

▲ Food is broken down further by digestive juices from the stomach and other organs such as the pancreas and gallbladder.

▲ By the time it reaches the intestines, your food is a soup of tiny nutrients. It passes through the walls of the intestines into the bloodstream.

◄ Every day, your body gets rid of waste products, such as undigested food and chemicals that the body does not need.

The brain and senses

The human brain has amazing powers. It makes sense of the world around us and helps us figure out how we can take part. It allows us to think complicated thoughts and explain complex ideas to other people and then tells us how to do what we need or want to do. There is no machine or computer that can match it.

Intelligent humans

As humans, we are such intelligent creatures that we can make use of the world around us more than any other living thing can. We succeed and survive all over the world, even in difficult conditions.

◀ Very few animals can use tools, but humans can make complex equipment to build, shape, and control the world. We can even learn to control airplanes and travel huge distances across the world.

▶ Human brains are larger than those of many other animals. An ape's head is similar in size to a human's, but our brains are about three times heavier. The parts that give us special abilities, such as language, emotions, and problem solving, are very well developed.

AMANING!

A human brain weighs about 46 oz. (1,300g), an ape's brain weighs about 11–18 oz. (300–500g), and a squirrel's brain weighs only 0.2 oz. (6g). Whales and dolphins have the next biggest brains after us relative to body size.

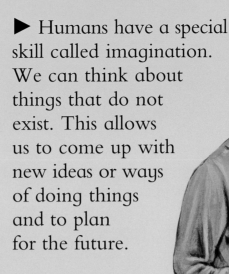

USING TOOLS

Fossils dug from the ground show that humans started using tools as long as three million years ago. These tools were sharpened stones used to cut up meat. We use much more complicated tools now.

▶ Humans have a special skill called imagination. We can think about things that do not exist. This allows us to come up with new ideas or ways of doing things and to plan for the future.

CREATIVE CORNER

Dream up your own house

Draw a picture of your dream house. Include all the special features that you would like it to have.

The nervous system

The nervous system is the most complex system in your body. It does thousands of different things all at the same time, sensing the world around you and sending instructions to every part of your body to keep it working as it should.

▶ The nervous system consists of two main parts. One is the control center of the body, which is made up of the brain and the spinal cord. The second part is the nerves, which carry electrical signals back and forth between the brain and the rest of the body.

AMAZING!
The nervous system works very quickly so that we can react fast when we need to. Signals can travel down a nerve at up to 217 mph (350km/h), faster than a sports car can drive.

spinal cord

nerve

VOCABULARY

spinal cord
The column of nerve tissue that runs from the brain down the back

synapse
The place where the end of a nerve cell connects with another cell

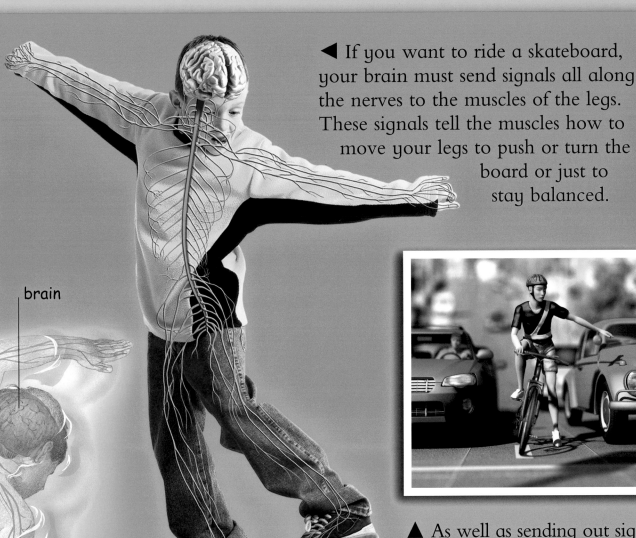

◀ If you want to ride a skateboard, your brain must send signals all along the nerves to the muscles of the legs. These signals tell the muscles how to move your legs to push or turn the board or just to stay balanced.

brain

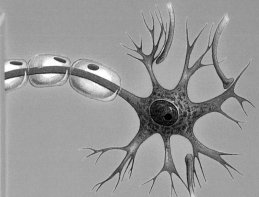

▲ As well as sending out signals to control the body, the brain also receives signals from the senses and the rest of the body, telling it what is going on in the world around it.

NERVE CONNECTIONS

Special structures called synapses join nerves to one another or to other cells, similar to how plugs and sockets join electrical wires. This means that messages can spread quickly to different areas of the body.

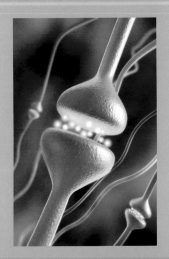

▲ Nerve cells are very thin and can be very long. Some stretch all the way from your big toe to your spine.

The brain is in control

Packed with billions of nerve cells, the brain is in charge of your body. It checks all the information from the sense organs, makes decisions about what to do, and then sends signals out to get things done.

AMAZING!
The brain can process and store huge amounts of information, but it needs a lot of energy to do this. Even though it makes up only about 2 percent of the body's weight, it uses up to 20 percent of its oxygen supply.

right side of the cerebrum

left side of the cerebrum

▼ The brain has two main parts called the cerebrum and the cerebellum. Different parts, or lobes, of the cerebrum are in control of different activities. The brain floats in fluid inside the hard, protective box of the skull.

cerebrum _____

cerebellum _____

◄ The cerebrum is divided vertically into two halves. The left side of the cerebrum controls the movement of the right side of the body, and the right side of it controls the movement of the left side of the body.

▶ As humans, we have special abilities to think, make choices, and control our bodies. We do not simply act like thoughtless zombies. We consider problems, take risks, achieve great things, and overcome problems through determination and willpower.

◀ The brain adjusts how your internal organs are working all the time without you knowing it. If you see something scary, it speeds up your heart, getting your body ready to escape.

CONTROL ROOM

Everything you do needs action from several different parts of the brain. As in a busy control room, messages whiz around from one part to another. Working together, all the parts of the brain can get the job done. This picture shows the busiest parts of the brain, at one particular moment, in green.

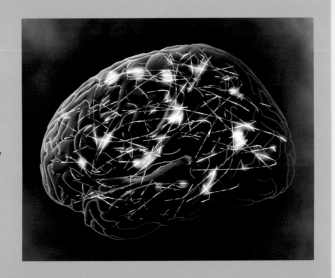

INTERNET LINKS: www.e-learningforkids.org/health/lesson/brain

Controlling movement

Your body almost never stops moving, and the brain is in charge of all this action. It controls everything from tiny hand movements when you write words to throwing your whole body around when you jump or dance.

▶ Different areas of the brain are in charge of different activities, although they all work together. Some parts deal with movement, some with information coming from the senses, and others with memory, speech, emotions, abstract thoughts, and problem solving.

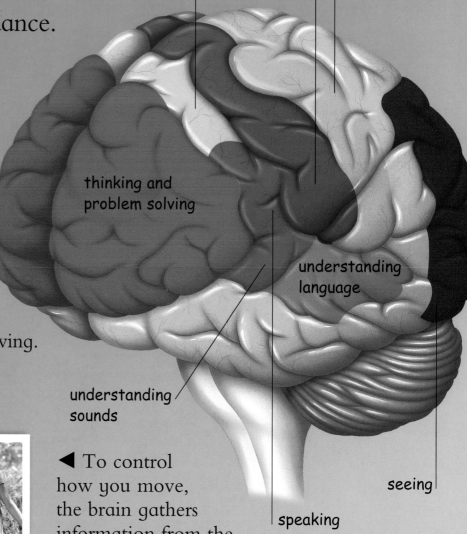

movement

touch and pain (skin senses)

coordinating movement

thinking and problem solving

understanding language

understanding sounds

seeing

speaking

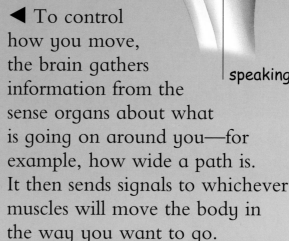

◀ To control how you move, the brain gathers information from the sense organs about what is going on around you—for example, how wide a path is. It then sends signals to whichever muscles will move the body in the way you want to go.

CREATIVE CORNER

Can you find the toys?

Your brain can move your body very precisely. Put some toys in front of you and look at them briefly. Now close your eyes and reach out for one. Even with your eyes shut, your brain can make you find and pick things up very easily.

▼ If the nerves in a person's spinal cord are damaged, signals may no longer get through from the brain to the muscles. The person cannot move freely anymore and may need a wheelchair to get around.

▶ Movement is important when we communicate. We move and shape our mouths to speak, but we also show how we feel with our face muscles, hands, heads, and bodies. What does this girl's body language tell us about how she feels?

BEAT THAT!

How fast can you text the sentence "The razor-toothed piranhas of the genera Serrasalmus and Pygocentrus are the most ferocious freshwater fish in the world. In reality they seldom attack a human."? The world record is 40.72 seconds.

INTERNET LINKS: http://faculty.washington.edu/chudler/interr.html

Sensing the world

We use our senses to help us get through the world and protect us from danger. When we see, hear, smell, taste, and touch what is around us, we send information to the brain that it can use to figure out what is happening outside the body.

▼ The brain combines signals from all your sense organs to build a picture of the world. Even if one sense, such as your sight, is not working, the other senses give the brain enough information so you can find your way around.

CAN YOU FIND?
1. Someone tasting
2. Someone hearing
3. Someone touching
4. Someone seeing

AMAZING!

Some people's senses are automatically mixed up. They experience color when they hear some sounds, or they taste certain foods when they read words. This strange condition is called synesthesia (sin-uhs-**thee**-zhuh).

◄ A human brain has many more connections between the nerves than other animal brains have. All these connections are very good at processing a lot of information from the sense organs.

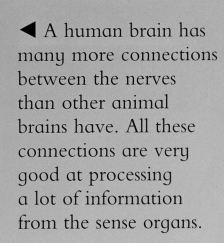

nerve

◄ What our eyes see affects how something tastes. Experiments show that if the color of a food is changed using food coloring, people say that it tastes different. Brightly colored foods often seem to taste better, while dark or strangely colored foods do not taste as good.

INTERNET LINKS: www.kids-science-experiments.com/cat_senses.html

How we see

Our eyes are the most complex sense organs in the body, giving us detailed pictures of the world around us. Sight is one of the most useful senses that we have. We often think using pictures in our mind and dream with pictures, too.

HOW DO GLASSES HELP?
Many people need glasses to help them see more clearly. Glasses work by helping the lens in the eye bend the light from an object, so that it focuses clearly on the retina.

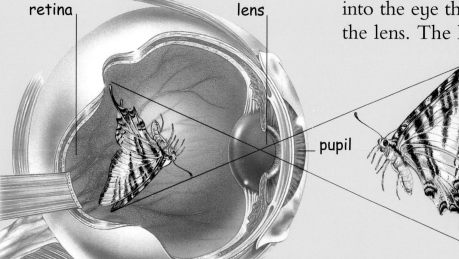

retina   lens

pupil

▼ Rays of light from an object pass into the eye through the pupil and reach the lens. The lens bends the light rays, turning them upside down and focusing them onto a special membrane at the back of the eye called the retina.

◄ The retina is packed with special sensors that are triggered when light hits them. They send signals to the brain, where the information is processed and the image is turned the right way up.

► Tiny muscles in the colored iris control the light that enters the eye. In bright light, the iris makes the pupil smaller, to protect the eye. If there is less light, the iris makes the pupil larger, allowing more light in and helping you see.

iris
pupil

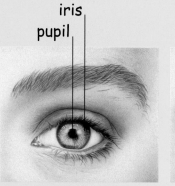

OPTICAL ILLUSIONS

Optical illusions are pictures that trick the brain. Here are two fun examples:

The lines below may look as if they zigzag, but if you measure them with a ruler, you will find that they are parallel!

Which of the middle circles below is bigger? Now measure them to check!

▲ Humans see the world in color and use this ability all the time to recognize objects, pick out ripe fruit, or simply to enjoy making colorful pictures.

▶ Most of the eyeball sits safely in a socket in the skull covered by the eyelid, which protects it from damage. Tears made by a gland above the eye wash across its surface and drain into the nose, keeping the eye free from dust.

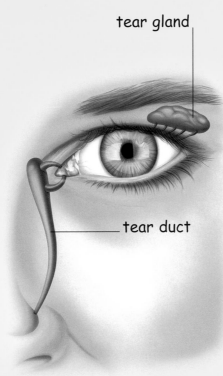

tear gland

tear duct

VOCABULARY

iris
The colored muscle around the pupil

lens
The clear structure behind the pupil that bends light

pupil
The opening in the center of the eye that light passes through

retina
The surface at the back of the eye that detects light

How we hear

110

Sounds make waves of pressure that travel through the air. We use our ears to receive these sound waves and turn them into sounds that we can understand. Hearing helps us communicate, warns us of dangers approaching, and allows us to enjoy music.

CAN YOU FIND?
1. A baby crying
2. Two women talking
3. A cat's ears
4. A dog barking
5. A plane flying
6. A car driving past

TURN IT DOWN
Very loud sounds can damage your ears and may eventually make you deaf. Always protect your ears in noisy places and keep the volume down when using music players. The top volume of a music player can be as noisy as a jet plane (a damaging 120 decibels).

▼ We hear many different sounds every day. Sound waves come from people talking and noisy traffic, for example. These sounds are collected by the outer flap of the ear, called the pinna.

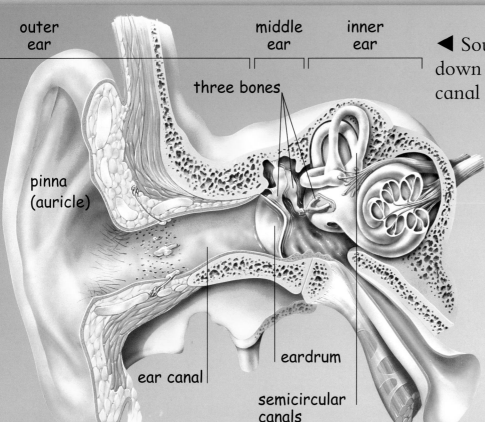

outer ear

middle ear

inner ear

three bones

pinna (auricle)

ear canal

eardrum

semicircular canals

◀ Sound waves pass down though the ear canal and hit the eardrum.

◀ The sound rattles the eardrum and shakes three bones in the middle ear. These bones act like drumsticks, beating on the outside of the inner ear, where the sound is turned into nerve signals that travel to the brain.

▲ If your hearing does not work well, you may need to use other ways to communicate. Some people use sign language to talk to those around them. Others use a hearing aid, a tiny device that fits into the ear to make sound louder and easier to hear.

CREATIVE CORNER

Test a friend's hearing

Ask a friend to close their eyes. Jingle some coins, clap your hands, tear up paper, scratch your head, and bounce a ball in front of them. What sounds do they recognize?

Balance

The brain gathers information from the sense organs to help us stay coordinated and balanced. Without balance, we could not stand upright.

HIGH-WIRE HELP

The acrobat at the bottom is holding a long, flexible pole to help him keep his balance on a narrow wire high up above the ground.

◀ To keep the body balanced on a surfboard, for example, the brain uses clues from what we can see around us and information from the balance organs in the inner ear. It also needs information from sensors in the muscles and joints to figure out what position the body is in.

▶ In the inner ear, there are three semicircular canals filled with liquid that sloshes around in different directions as we move. These tell the brain how the head is turning, or rotating. The structures in the inner ear work together to send nerve signals to the brain about our position and movement.

▲ Turn back to page 111 to see the semicircular canals in the inner ear.

CREATIVE CORNER

Test your sense of balance

See what happens if you lose your sense of balance. Find some flat ground with a lot of space so you will not hurt yourself if you fall. Spin around ten times and then stop and try to walk in a straight line.

▲ A lot of movement in different directions can upset the brain and make you feel dizzy and sick. Fixing your sight on something that is not moving, such as the horizon, can help the brain figure out where the body is and control motion sickness.

INTERNET LINKS: www.childrenfirst.nhs.uk/kids/health/body_tour/ears.html

Smell and taste

Smell and taste work together to sense chemicals in the air around us and in the food we eat. This helps us enjoy food and makes us want to eat. These senses also warn us of danger. Smell and taste tell us if food is spoiled, and our sense of smell alone picks up the smell of smoke from a fire.

▼ You can recognize many flowers by their scents. If you take a deep breath in, chemical molecules given off by a flower drift up into the nose and trigger sensors, sending signals that the brain can identify.

taste sensor

nerve carries signals to brain

smell sensors

smell molecules are breathed in through the nose

▲ When you taste something, taste sensors (taste buds) on your tongue sense chemical molecules in the food. Your sense of taste is not as sensitive as your sense of smell, however. It can tell the difference only between five main types of taste—sweet, salty, sour, bitter, and a meaty taste known as umami.

▲ Perfumers carefully select and mix dozens of smells from about 3,000 possible ingredients when they make new perfumes. It takes many years to learn how to do this.

SMELLY FEET

Humans have smell sensors in their noses, but other animals have them in more unusual places. Butterflies have sense organs on their feet that allow them to taste the leaves they stand on to see if they are suitable food for their caterpillars.

▲ When you have a cold, you cannot taste things very well. This is because a large part of how your brain detects taste is through smell. Having a stuffed nose stops the air carrying smells from reaching your smell sensors.

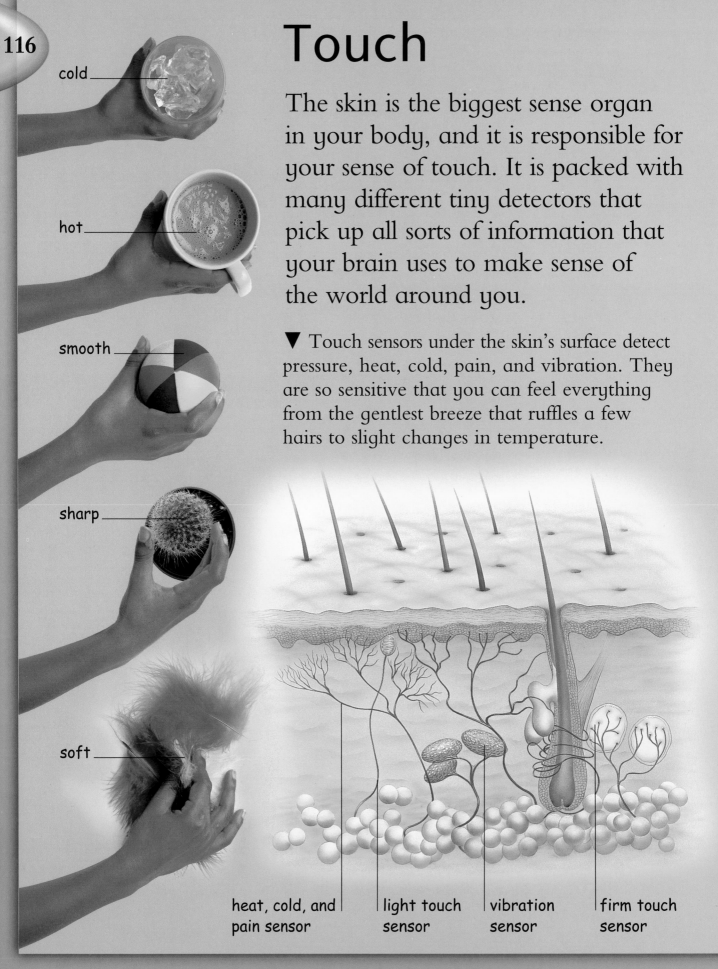

cold

hot

smooth

sharp

soft

Touch

The skin is the biggest sense organ in your body, and it is responsible for your sense of touch. It is packed with many different tiny detectors that pick up all sorts of information that your brain uses to make sense of the world around you.

▼ Touch sensors under the skin's surface detect pressure, heat, cold, pain, and vibration. They are so sensitive that you can feel everything from the gentlest breeze that ruffles a few hairs to slight changes in temperature.

heat, cold, and pain sensor

light touch sensor

vibration sensor

firm touch sensor

► Some parts of the body, such as the fingers and tongue, have more touch sensors and are more sensitive than others. This is what your body would look like if the different parts were in proportion to the number of sensors they contain.

BRAILLE

Braille is a system of reading and writing that uses raised dots on paper instead of printed words. Blind people can use Braille to read by feeling the patterns of dots with their fingers.

WHY DO BABIES PUT OBJECTS IN THEIR MOUTHS?

Lips contain many touch sensors. Babies like to use them to feel and find out about objects around them.

► Touch is important because it warns us about things that might damage the body, but it can also give us pleasure. You can enjoy holding a soft teddy bear, wrapping yourself in a fluffy blanket, or walking barefoot on a smooth floor because of your sense of touch.

Reflexes and reactions

Sometimes your body reacts to something automatically, without your even having to think about it. These quick movements are called reflexes, and they protect your body from harm.

AMAZING!
If a ball comes flying at your face, a protective reflex makes your eyelids blink shut quickly. You may even scrunch up your eyes or bring your hands up to your face for extra protection.

◀ If you touch something hot or sharp, you automatically pull your hand away. This happens even before your brain has received information from the sense organs that there is a problem. This is called the withdrawal reflex.

▶ Many reflexes are controlled by the spinal cord. Signals travel to it along nerves from sense organs in the skin. Even before the information reaches the brain, a signal zaps back out from the spinal cord that tells the muscles to move.

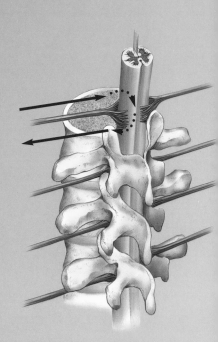

▲ Athletes need good reflexes. Runners and swimmers need to react quickly to the starting pistol, while tennis players may have less than half a second to react to a ball coming their way.

▲ Sneezing and coughing are also types of reflexes. The body uses them to clear dust and particles out of the airways. Once you feel that you are about to sneeze, it is difficult to stop it!

A BABY'S REFLEXES

Babies are born with many reflexes that they need to survive. They automatically root around to find their mother's breast to feed. They also grab anything placed in their hands, such as a finger. If they are dropped suddenly, they automatically stretch out their arms as if to break their fall.

INTERNET LINKS: http://kidshealth.org/kid/talk/qa/reflexes.html

Emotions and memory

As humans, we like to live in groups. We enjoy laughing and joking together and sharing our good experiences. This helps us feel closer to one another. We often feel better when we share bad feelings, too.

AMAZING!
Some people have incredible memories, remembering events or facts in great detail. A few of them may have an extra-special brain, but most have simply worked hard to develop their memory skills—and you can, too!

▼ Every day, you probably feel many different emotions, from happiness and amusement to fear, worry, anger, and even sadness. We all feel these emotions in our minds, and our bodies also show them. We can shake with fear, roll around with laughter, and curl up and cry with unhappiness.

PHOBIAS

Fear is a very useful emotion. It helps the body stay away from things that could harm it. However, many people develop fears of things such as spiders that they do not really need to be afraid of. These fears are called phobias.

▲ Your brain has an amazing ability to store information and then use it when needed. This is called memory, and it plays a very important role in learning and intelligence. We need memory for the simplest of tasks, as well as more complex skills such as riding a bicycle.

▼ The same part of your brain controls both emotions and memories. This may explain why memories of things that happened a long time ago can still make you emotional and why certain emotions can stir up memories.

INTERNET LINKS: www.playkidsgames.com/memoryGames.htm

Intelligence

Humans are very intelligent for several reasons. Our brains store and process information very well, and we can also think abstract thoughts, which helps us solve problems and adapt to new conditions.

▶ Humans like to invent things. We come up with new ideas all the time, using modern designs and technology to make things to help us do jobs better. Inventing better buildings, machines, and communication systems helps us survive.

AMAZING!

If you take care of your body, you will also be taking care of your brain and improving your intelligence. A healthy diet, plenty of exercise, and regular sleep are as important to your brain as they are for the rest of your body.

▶ When you try to answer a question or make a plan, you use the front part of the brain, called the frontal lobes. You also use the outer surface of the brain, called the cortex, which is often known as your "gray matter."

frontal lobes

BRAINTEASERS

You can improve your brainpower by challenging yourself every day with problem-solving games. Word puzzles, memory games, brainteasers, and games such as chess all make the millions of connections in your brain stronger.

▶ Most animals can communicate in some way, but only humans use such complex languages. We can describe things in very precise ways and share detailed thoughts with others, and this helps us work better together.

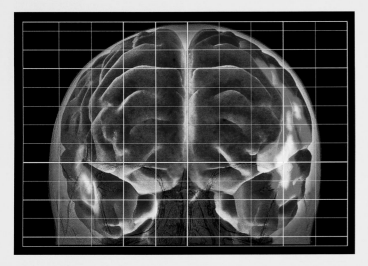

◀ Special scans provide very detailed pictures of the structure of the brain, while others show the blood supply or which parts of the brain are working at any one time. This scan shows how the brain works when we read. The areas that are being used appear in yellow.

Sleep

You may think that your brain turns off when you sleep. In fact, it is still very busy. Scientists cannot say exactly why we all need sleep, but we must have it. It seems that the brain uses that time to sort out information it received while you were awake.

?

IS TAKING A NAP GOOD FOR YOU?
Napping suits some people, but others prefer only to sleep at night. A short nap can help to restore energy levels and make you feel refreshed.

▶ Newborn babies sleep on and off all day, for 16 hours or more. They slowly get into a routine, and once children are in school they mainly just sleep through the night. Adults need much less sleep than children do.

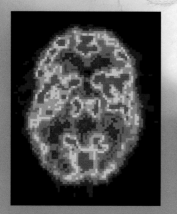

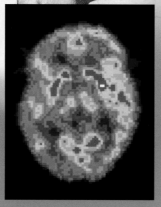

Light, REM sleep   Deep sleep

◀ While you sleep, electrical activity in the brain, known as brain waves, changes. These scans show, in red, the parts of the brain that are active during light, rapid eye movement (REM) sleep and the parts that are active during deep sleep. The brain is more active in light, REM sleep.

▼ Something else happens while you sleep. A small gland at the base of the brain, called the pituitary gland, releases a lot of a chemical signal, called a growth hormone, that makes you grow. So it is very important to get a good night's sleep.

pituitary gland

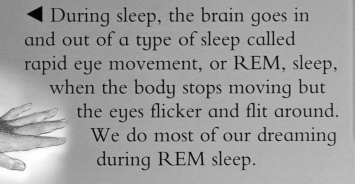

◀ During sleep, the brain goes in and out of a type of sleep called rapid eye movement, or REM, sleep, when the body stops moving but the eyes flicker and flit around. We do most of our dreaming during REM sleep.

BREATHING UNDERWATER

Bottlenose dolphins spend their entire lives in the water, so how do they sleep without drowning? While they sleep, they shut down only half of their brain. The other half stays awake and controls their breathing through a blowhole. After about two hours, the other side of the brain takes over.

◀ Sometimes people get up and move around while sleeping. This is called sleepwalking, and it is quite common, especially in young children. A person may simply sit up and look around or do more complex things such as getting dressed or even eating food. No one knows why this happens.

INTERNET LINKS: www.sleepforkids.org/index.html

The artificial brain

For more than 50 years, humans have been building artificial brains, or computers. We continue to build more and more powerful ones and find uses for them in every area of life, but none yet combines all the skills and powers of the human mind.

COMPUTER POWER

Most modern cars have a computer system that is more powerful than the one that guided astronauts to the Moon in 1969.

◀ Scientists can now build computerized robots that walk and talk like humans. This robot, called Asimo, can avoid obstacles, climb stairs, and hold objects. It can recognize faces and respond to simple commands, so it can help carry out various tasks.

▲ Computers can store figures, facts, and pictures, but they cannot understand behavior and emotions as humans can. So while computers are useful for creating the pictures in animated movies, such as *Toy Story*, it takes a human to create the story in the first place.

◀ You can find computers in every part of daily life now, running the washing machine, at the supermarket checkout, and inside cars. You probably use one when you play computer games, of course, but there are many others.

▶ Robots are human-made machines with similar parts to humans, including a body with movable joints, a sensory system to collect information, and a computer "brain" to control them. We use robots to do many precise or repetitive jobs, such as making cars.

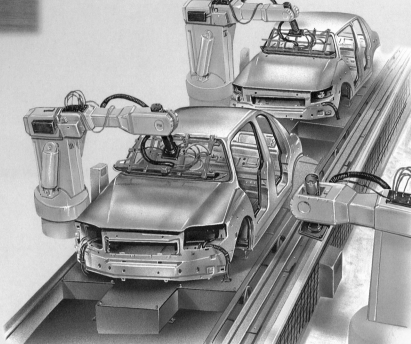

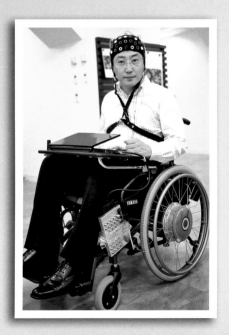

◀ Special devices using artificial intelligence can now help people with all sorts of diseases and disabilities. Heart pacemakers check the heartbeat of a person with heart disease, and there are computerized wheelchairs to help paralyzed people move around more easily.

AMAZING!
Computer power is increasing at a very fast rate. Experts think that computers will overtake humans in their brainpower by the 2020s.

Now you know!

◄ The human brain is larger (compared to our body size) and more powerful than that of any other animal.

► Different parts of the brain control different activities, including movement, speech, balance, and memory.

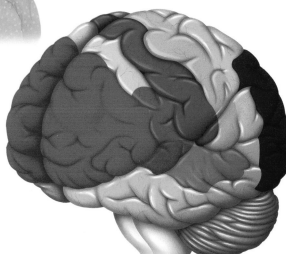

▲ The nervous system, which includes the brain and nerves, is in charge of everything we feel and do.

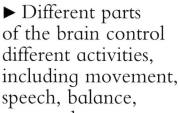

▲ The brain collects information about the world around us through the sense organs, including our eyes, ears, nose, and skin.

▼ Messages go to and from the brain very quickly along nerves. At times, our bodies move without us even thinking about it.

▲ Humans can feel many emotions. We also have a powerful memory.

► We are very intelligent animals. We use our brains to solve many problems, and we can build intelligent machines, or robots, too.

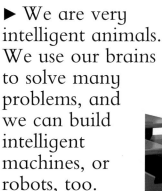

▲ While we sleep, the brain is busy making sense of information that we received while we were awake.

Structure and movement

No animal has a body quite like a human's or moves in the same way. Our light, flexible skeleton allows us to walk on just two legs, leaving our arms and hands free to use tools. Our upright structure is one of the reasons why humans have been so successful on Earth.

Standing and moving

Humans can move in many
different ways. We can stand on
two legs, run, bend down, and
crawl on all fours, or even swim
to get to where we want to go.

▼ We are one of the few animals to move
on two legs, leaving our hands free to do
other things. Some animals, such as meerkats,
stand upright for a short while when they are
looking for enemies, and others do so to eat
or fight. Most other animals need to use their
upper or front limbs when they move.

STANDING ON ONE LEG

When we
stand on two
legs, we have
to adjust our
posture all the time
to stay balanced.
Standing on one leg
is even harder. The
record for doing this is
76 hours and 40 minutes,
set by Arulanantham
Suresh Joachim in
Sri Lanka in 1997.

131

▲ Our hands are free to build and shape what we need. This sculptor grips and moves the tools with his hands when he carves a statue. If he needed to stand on all four limbs, he would not be able to do this.

CREATIVE CORNER

Using arms for speed

Moving our arms can make us faster when we run. First, race a friend with your arms folded across your chest. Then race again, pumping your arms back and forth. Do you run faster this time?

AMAZING!

Humans love to show what their bodies can do. In competitions such as the Olympic Games, people from around the world compete against one another in sports that demonstrate almost every way that humans can move.

▲ Our bodies are very flexible. We can bend over, twist and turn our bodies and limbs, and move in many different ways. Gymnasts make the most of their flexibility when they perform.

The skeleton

The skeleton is a strong, bony frame that holds up the body and keeps its shape. The hard bones protect delicate organs, while joints between them make the skeleton able to move. Without a skeleton, we would simply be wobbly lumps of soft tissue.

▼ The skeleton is made of 206 different bones of all shapes and sizes. Some bones, such as in the arms and legs, are long and thin, while those in the skull, for example, are like flat plates. The hands and feet contain groups of much smaller bones.

AMAZING!
It is not unusual to have extra bones somewhere in the skeleton. About one in 500 people has an extra rib in the neck, at the top of the rib cage above the normal first rib. This does not usually cause them any problems.

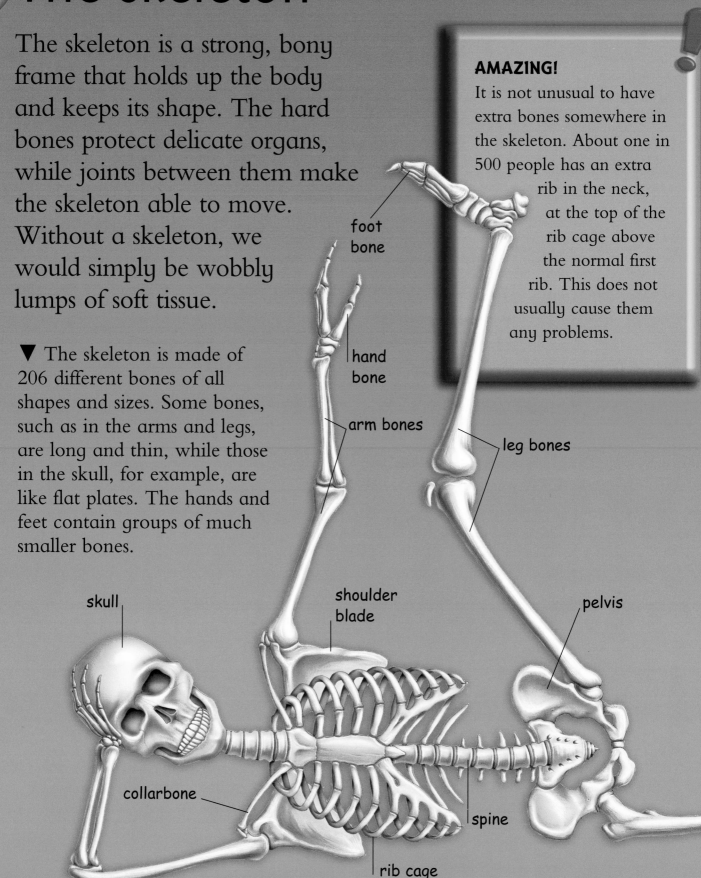

foot bone

hand bone

arm bones

leg bones

skull

shoulder blade

pelvis

collarbone

spine

rib cage

THE SIGN FOR DANGER

All around the world, people use skeletons as symbols of death, disease, or danger. A skull and crossbones is often used as a warning sign on poisonous substances, and years ago, pirates used it to show that they were a danger to other sailing ships.

▶ Animals have similar types of bones to us, but the size or shape of their bones makes their bodies look different to ours. Giraffes have exactly the same number of bones in their necks as we do, but the bones are much larger, so their necks are very long.

133

◀ The center of the skeleton is the spine and the ribs. The arms are connected to the spine by a bony ring made of the collarbones and shoulder blades. The legs are attached to it by a ring of bones called the pelvis. The ribs form a cage that protects important organs, such as the heart and lungs.

◀ We use our muscles to pull our skeleton into a shape, or posture. If we stand up straight, the muscles and bones can work well together. A bad posture, such as sitting with hunched shoulders, can eventually harm the bones and tissues.

INTERNET LINKS: www.e-learningforkids.org/health/lesson/skeleton

Bones

Your bones feel hard and can be as strong as steel, but they are made of living tissue, full of cells and protein. They are slightly flexible and springy, which helps them stand up to knocks and bumps.

▶ Every bone, like this leg bone, for example, is covered by a thin protective membrane. Just beneath this is the toughest part of the bone, made from bundles of long, bony tubes. Bone cells in the tubes build up layers of protein and a hard mineral called calcium to make the bone strong.

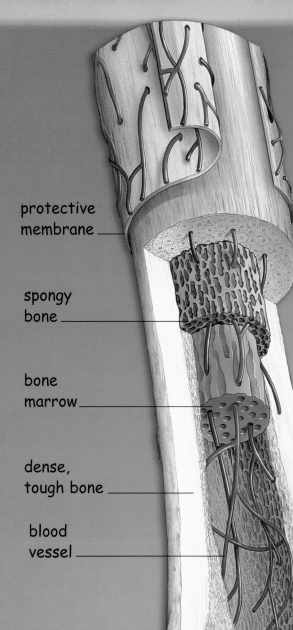

protective membrane

spongy bone

bone marrow

dense, tough bone

blood vessel

GET ON YOUR FEET!

Regular exercise helps keep bones healthy. Playing sports where you stand on your feet and let your bones carry the weight of your body, such as basketball, is especially good for making your bones stronger.

◀ Further inside, the bone is spongy, with a network of columns and air spaces. This helps keep bones light. The spaces in the center of many bones are filled with a soft substance called marrow, which makes red blood cells.

▲ To help your bones grow strong, you need a lot of calcium in your diet. Dairy products, such as milk and cheese, as well as eggs, many fish, and green vegetables have a lot of calcium.

AMAZING!

By looking at a skeleton, scientists can figure out the age of the person it belonged to. Over the years, bones grow, harden, fuse together, and change shape, getting more ragged. It is these signs that show how old a bone is.

▲ As people grow older, they may lose calcium from their bones, which makes them weaker and more likely to break. It is very important that older people exercise to strengthen their muscles and their sense of balance so that they are less likely to fall over.

The spine and ribs

The spine, or backbone, is a column of small bones piled one on top of another, with the skull at the top. These bones, plus the surrounding muscles and ligaments, form your back. You can feel the bumpy bones of your spine if you rub your fingers up and down the middle of your back.

▼ There are 24 bones, or vertebrae, in your spine. A further seven vertebrae are joined together at the bottom of the spine to form part of the pelvis.

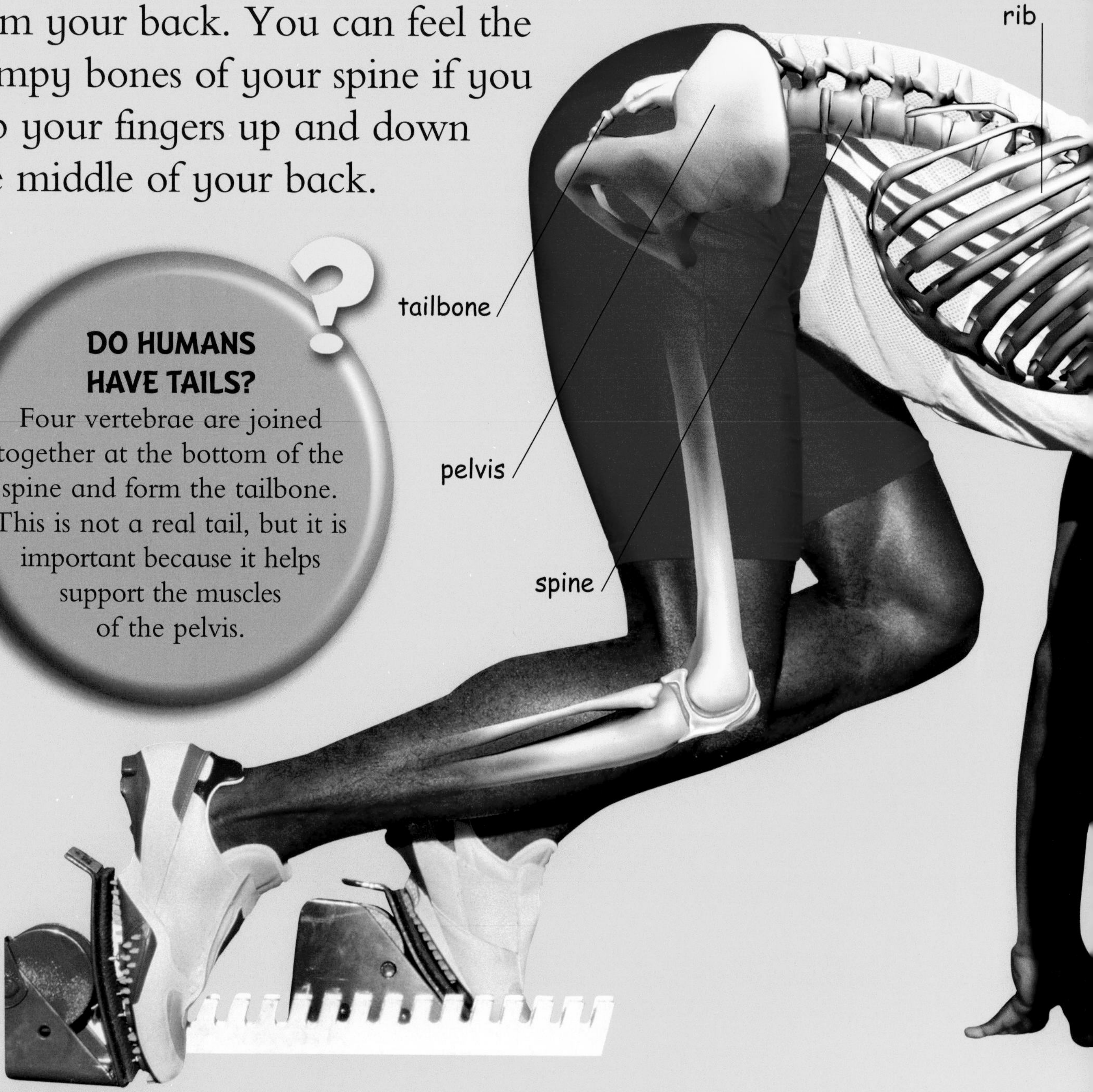

rib

DO HUMANS HAVE TAILS?

Four vertebrae are joined together at the bottom of the spine and form the tailbone. This is not a real tail, but it is important because it helps support the muscles of the pelvis.

tailbone

pelvis

spine

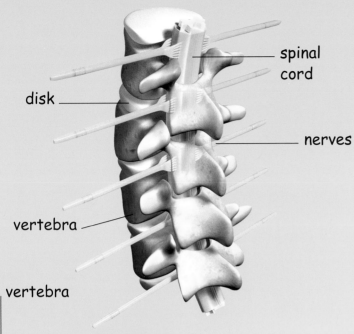

disk

spinal cord

nerves

vertebra

vertebra

skull

▲ Each vertebra is shaped a little like a knobby ring. The vertebrae, lined up together, form a bony tunnel, and the delicate nervous tissue of the spinal cord runs through it. Between each vertebra, a spongy disk acts as a shock absorber, protecting the spine from damage when you move.

◄ Twelve pairs of thin bones called ribs are attached to the vertebrae high up on the spine. They curve around to join the bony breastbone at the front of the chest and form a cage to protect the lungs and heart.

► The bones of the spine are not a straight column but form a gentle S-shaped curve. This helps make it very springy and flexible, allowing you to bend and stretch your back.

The skull

Twenty-two bones are joined together to form the skull, which gives shape to your head and face. One of the skull's most important jobs is to protect the brain, the most delicate organ of the body, and all the nerves that go in and out of it.

▶ The main part of the skull is made of plates of bone locked tightly together like the pieces of a jigsaw puzzle. These form a bony box to hold the brain. The skull is rigid and strong and is able to resist quite heavy bumps.

WHY IS THE HOLE FOR THE NOSE SO LARGE?
Although your nose feels solid, it is made of a substance called cartilage, not bone, which breaks down when we die, revealing the large hole in our skull.

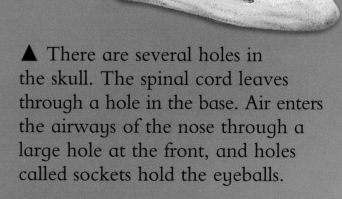

▲ There are several holes in the skull. The spinal cord leaves through a hole in the base. Air enters the airways of the nose through a large hole at the front, and holes called sockets hold the eyeballs.

▶ The only bone in the skull that can move is the lower jawbone. This is attached to the rest of the skull on both sides, so it can move up and down when we chew food with our teeth and lets us move our mouths when we talk.

◀ Scientists can now figure out what a dead person once looked like from the remains of their skull. They can attach muscles made of clay to the bone to rebuild the face. This has been done to certain ancient Egyptian mummies, so now we have a clearer idea of how some of the pharaohs looked.

PROTECTING THE BRAIN

Even though the skull does a good job protecting the brain, head injuries still cause brain damage to thousands of people every year. We can give the skull extra help by wearing a helmet when we do sports such as cycling and skateboarding.

INTERNET LINKS: www.ehow.com/facts_5591777_human-skull-kids.html

Arms and hands

We use our arms and hands almost every minute of the day to put on clothes, play with toys, pick up food, type on the computer, or simply to balance as we move around. Without them, life would be very difficult.

GET A GRIP!

Your fingertips are covered with a pattern of tiny ridges on the skin that help you grip. Each finger has its own unique pattern that you leave behind as a fingerprint on everything you touch.

SENSITIVE FINGERS

Our fingertips are packed with sensory nerves, making our hands very impressive tools. We can feel tiny changes in the surface of an object. We can also make tiny, accurate movements, allowing us to do complicated tasks, such as playing musical instruments.

◀ The hand is very flexible because it is formed of so many small bones. They allow the hand to wrap tightly around an object and grip it securely, curl to form a cup to catch water, or stretch the long fingers to make shapes with the finger and thumb.

▲ We can move the thumb in a different way from the other fingers. If we bring it to meet the fingertips, we can grip tiny objects. This "opposable thumb" is very useful and makes humans very successful animals.

CREATIVE CORNER

Opposable thumbs

Try doing things without your opposable thumbs. Put on a pair of gloves but leave your thumbs in the palms of your hands inside the gloves. Now try to pick up a knife and fork or put building bricks together.

◀ The arms hang down from the shoulders on either side of the body. Each arm has three long bones and 27 small bones grouped together at the end to form the hand. These bones allow us to move our arms in many directions: to pull, push, pick up, and throw.

▲ If someone loses a leg in an accident, doctors can replace it with an artificial one. Modern artificial legs are amazing. They can look like real legs and can do many of the same jobs.

INTERNET LINKS: www.cyh.com/HealthTopics/HealthTopicDetailsKids.aspx?p=335&np=152&id=2458

Legs and feet

Our legs are bigger and stronger than our arms because they have to carry the full weight of the body when we move. Large, powerful leg muscles allow us to walk and run and can push the whole body off the ground when we jump.

AMAZING!

Having big feet can be an advantage in some sports. Size-17 feet helped Australian swimmer Ian Thorpe win five Olympic gold medals and 13 world records. Like a seal's flippers, these unusually large feet powered his body through the water!

▶ The legs are joined to the skeleton at the bony ring called the pelvis. They are formed by three long bones, with a group of small bones in the feet. There is an extra small, round bone over the knee joint called the kneecap.

▶ The thighbone joins the hip to the knee. It is the largest bone in the body and also one of the strongest. Working with powerful muscles in the thigh and buttock, this bone can support up to 30 times a person's weight.

leg bones

FOOTPRINT FACTS

Dinosaur footprints left behind in mud or volcanic ash can still be seen today. Scientists study them to figure out which dinosaurs existed in a particular area and how long ago. A few ancient human footprints have been left behind for us to wonder about and investigate, too.

thighbone

kneecap

foot bones

▶ Strong tissues called ligaments hold the bones of the foot together and pull it up off the ground into an arched shape. Arches make the feet very springy, so they can push the body off the ground and move it forward. If you look at footprints on a sandy beach, you can see where the arch is in the center of the foot.

◀ Our feet form a platform that helps the body stay balanced and upright. They move differently from the hands, bending at the ankles and toes to push the body off the ground when we walk, run, or jump.

INTERNET LINKS: www.cyh.com/HealthTopics/HealthTopicDetailsKids.aspx?p=335&np=152&id=2340

Joints

Joints connect two bones. There are different kinds of joints. Flexible joints allow the skeleton to bend, twist, and turn. There are also some rigid joints, such as in the pelvis, where bones are locked solidly together to protect or support the body.

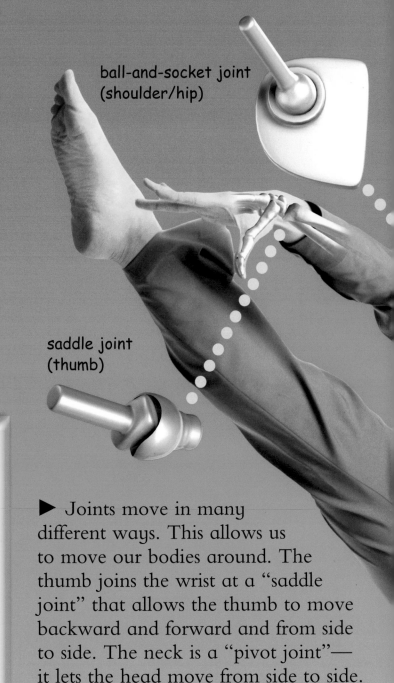

ball-and-socket joint
(shoulder/hip)

saddle joint
(thumb)

DOUBLE-JOINTED

Some very flexible people, like the girl below, are said to be "double-jointed." They do not really have extra joints. They simply have stretchier ligaments, so they can bend their joints farther than most other people can.

▶ Joints move in many different ways. This allows us to move our bodies around. The thumb joins the wrist at a "saddle joint" that allows the thumb to move backward and forward and from side to side. The neck is a "pivot joint"— it lets the head move from side to side.

▶ In some joints, such as the hips and shoulders, the round end of one bone fits into a hole (or socket) in another bone. These "ball-and-socket joints" allow you to move your legs and arms forward, backward, and around in circles.

pivot joint
(neck)

AMAZING!

As we get older, our joints often become damaged, especially the hips and knees, which carry the weight of the body. Every year, thousands of people have new artificial joints put in, which help them stay active for longer than they could naturally.

▶ Ligaments hold two bones together at a joint and keep the skeleton connected. Without ligaments, the bones would separate, and if you hung from a branch, for example, your arms would come apart from your body.

hinge joint
(knee/elbow)

◀ The knee and elbow are hinge joints—they can bend only up and down. Like many other joints where there is a lot of movement, the ends of the bones are covered in a hard, slippery tissue called cartilage. A hinge joint is filled with fluid to help the bones slide past each other easily.

INTERNET LINKS: www.childrenfirst.nhs.uk/kids/health/body_tour/bones_joints.php

Muscles

More than half the body is made from muscles. Their main job is to move the body. Every single movement we make needs muscle power to get it started. Muscles also support the skeleton and hold our shape, or posture.

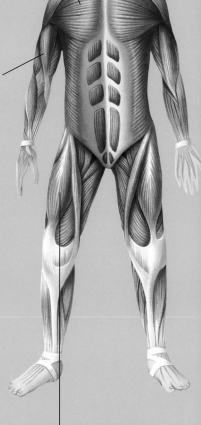

this muscle lets you smile

chest muscles pull your arms to your sides

biceps muscle bends your arm

thigh muscle straightens the knee

AMAZING!

There are more than 650 muscles in the body. The largest, called the gluteus maximus, forms the round shape of your bottom and helps move your legs. One of the smallest, in your ear, is just one millimeter long.

▶ Muscles are formed from sheets of muscle fibers lying together like ropes. Although we cannot see them under the skin, they give us our shape. Artists often study them for years to learn how to draw the human body.

◀ Most muscles are attached to bones, which they pull into position. To lift a weight, for example, muscles in the arms contract, or shorten, pulling up the arm bones. Many muscles in the face are attached to the skin and pull it around to make us smile or frown.

▼ Many muscles quietly do their jobs without our noticing them. The colored part of the eye, the iris, for example, is a muscle. It opens the pupil automatically to let more light in and closes it to stop too much from getting in.

CREATIVE CORNER

Feel your muscles in action

Hold your arm out straight and place your hand on the top surface of your upper arm. Now bend your arm up. You should feel the biceps muscle shortening, or contracting, to form a lump under your hand.

MUSCLES MAKE HEAT

Your muscles help keep your body warm. When you get very cold the muscles can start to work overtime, contracting and relaxing very quickly to burn energy and make heat. This is called shivering.

▶ Muscles are joined to bones by thick, fibrous tissues called tendons. You can feel one, called the Achilles tendon, at the back of your leg, just above your heel. This connects the calf muscle to the foot, pulling up the heel as you walk.

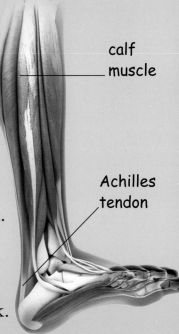

calf muscle

Achilles tendon

INTERNET LINKS: http://kids.discovery.com/tell-me/science/body-systems/your-muscular-system

Tough bones

Our bones are packed with calcium that helps make them tough and strong. They carry us around every day, taking the stresses and strains that we put on our body as we go about our lives.

broken bone

► Although bones are tough, they can break —for example, in an accident while playing or doing sports. A special scan called an x-ray can be used to check whether a bone is broken.

► A broken bone must be held in position for several weeks while the break heals. It is wrapped in a special bandage that sets rock hard. These bandages are known as casts.

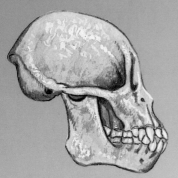 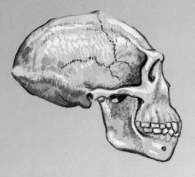 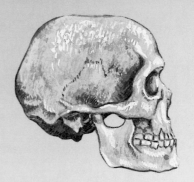

250,000,000 years old   1,000,000 years old   50,000 years old

AMAZING!

Bones are very slow to heal. A broken arm may take as long as six weeks or more and a broken leg even longer—up to ten or 12 weeks. During this time, they must be kept still in a cast.

▲ Tough bones stay behind long after an animal has died, giving scientists many clues about the past. By studying skulls like these of our human ancestors, it is possible to see how humans have changed over millions of years, from apes into you and me.

BONESETTERS

Long before modern hospitals and x-rays, people realized that broken bones needed to be set back into the right position in order to keep a person as active as possible. In medieval times, young boys could train to be a "bonesetter."

▲ The bones of ancient people, such as Egyptian mummies, tell scientists all sorts of things about how people used to live, what they ate, what diseases they had, and even what medicines they used.

Sports

There are hundreds of different sports to try, and almost all of them rely on the body's ability to move itself or change its shape. Some sports, such as running, need the body to move fast, while others, such as archery, rely on slow, precise movements.

◀ Before you start an activity, you usually need to do what is called "warming up." You gently stretch the muscles that you are going to use and start to increase the blood and oxygen supply to them, getting them ready for action.

▶ To be good at a sport, you must be in shape. This means being strong and flexible and having the power to keep going, which is called stamina. Different sports need these in different amounts. A marathon runner requires great stamina, while a rower needs strength, too.

◄ In yoga and gymnastics, being flexible is very important to help bend and shape the body. Some people are naturally more flexible than others, but you can become more flexible by stretching your muscles regularly.

HOW CAN YOU BE GOOD AT SPORTS?

To be good at sports, you need to practice regularly. You also need to eat a healthy, balanced diet and get plenty of rest.

DOING SPORTS

Some people enjoy taking part in competitions and winning prizes when they do sports. However, there are plenty of sports that are not competitive and that you can do simply for fun.

▲ During exercise, your heart beats faster and breathing becomes deeper in order to send enough nutrients and oxygen to the muscles. You also feel hot, as this special scan shows (the red areas of the body are the hottest). Your skin becomes red and you sweat to help cool down the body.

Remarkable movers

152

The body can move in such amazing ways that we use this ability to entertain others—in dance or in sports such as gymnastics, for example. Some movements the body makes are so tiny, hidden, or unexpected, however, that we do not even realize that they are happening inside us.

WHAT MOVEMENTS CAN YOU SOMETIMES FEEL IN YOUR BELLY?
These are waves of muscular contractions along the intestines that push food through the digestive system.

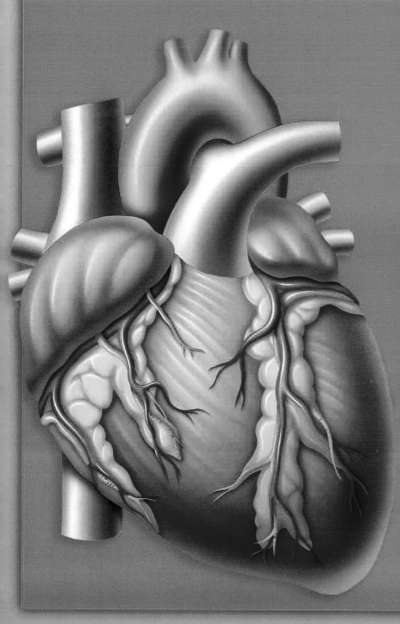

◀ Every second of every day, the muscles of your heart are contracting to squeeze blood around the body. Most of the time, you do not notice this movement, but if you make your heart beat very fast by running around, you may feel it thumping in your chest.

▲ Hundreds of times a day, we close our eyelids without thinking about it. This is called blinking, and it spreads tears across the eyes.

▲ Dancers know how to move their bodies to tell stories and show emotions. When a group of dancers all move together in time with the music, the effect can be very dramatic. Synchronized swimmers do the same—but in the water!

AMAZING!

Tiny muscles control the hairs on the skin, making them stand up on end when it is cold, like a small forest that traps air and provides a layer of insulation.

SINGING MUSCLES

To sing well, a singer needs to work the muscles that control the voice box and also those that control the lungs and breathing. A singer needs to hold his or her body in a good posture, too. Singing needs muscles!

▲ A drummer has to work his or her body as hard as an athlete, moving the arms very fast, sometimes for hours at a time. A drummer also has to create exciting rhythms. It is a great workout for the brain, nerves, and muscles!

INTERNET LINKS: www.kidzworld.com/article/5345-aerobics-101

Now you know!

◄ Inside the human body is a bony skeleton that gives us our shape. We can move on two feet, leaving our arms free to use tools.

◄ Although bone is very tough, it is a living tissue. If a bone breaks, the tissues can join up and heal again.

► There are hundreds of bones in the body of different shapes and sizes, linked by flexible joints so that we can bend and move in many ways.

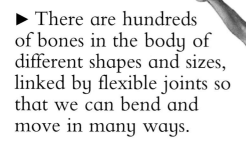

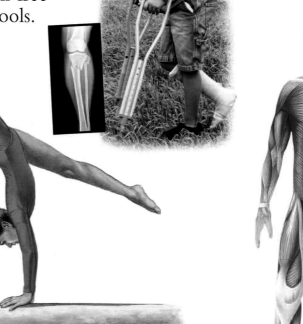

◄ Some parts of the skeleton, such as the skull and ribs, form hard boxes or cages to protect the soft, delicate organs inside.

▲ Hundreds of muscles pull the skeleton around to move the body.

▼ We can control our movements and our muscles very precisely. This allows us to play different sports and musical instruments.

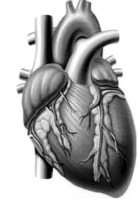

◄ The body never stops moving. Even while we sleep, our chests move as we breathe and our hearts beat, pumping blood around the body.

Index

Acknowledgments

The publisher would like to thank Wendy Burford at the Science Museum, London, U.K., and Graham Neale.

The publisher would like to thank the following for permission to reproduce their material.
Every care has been taken to trace copyright holders. However, if there have been unintentional
omissions or failure to trace copyright holders, we apologize and will, if informed,
endeavor to make corrections in any future edition.

top = t; bottom = b; center = c; left = l; right = r

Pages 6, 12, 14, 15, 17 Shutterstock; 22 Alamy/Phototake; 23, 25, 31cr, 31b, 35 Shutterstock; 36 Science Photo Library/Bluestone;
37l, 37r, 41, 43t, 43c, 44, 45t, 45b, 49t, 50, 51t, 51c Shutterstock; 51b Getty Images/Design; 53c, 53b, 55l, 55r, 56 Shutterstock;
57 Alamy/Miriam Reik; 58, 59tl, 59tr, 59cl, 59bl, 60, 61l, 61r, 63t, 63b, 67, 69, 73b, 74l, 74r, 75, 76l, 76r, 79cr, 79bl, 80, 81,
85 Shutterstock; 87c Getty Images/Science Photo Library; 87b Shutterstock; 88 Getty Images/Stockbyte; 89 Science Photo
Library/Y. Beaulieu/Publiphoto Diffusion; 91t, 91cr, 91b, 92–93, 93tl, 93c, 93b, 94tr, 94c, 101bl, 103cl Shutterstock;
103b Science Photo Library; 104, 105cr, 105bl, 105br, 107, 110, 111, 112, 113, 114 Shutterstock; 115 Corbis/Laurent Giraudon;
117, 119l, 119r, 121 Shutterstock; 122 Alamy/AF Archive; 123t, 123cr Shutterstock; 123b Science Photo Library/Sovereign ISM;
124l Science Photo Library/Hank Morgan; 124c Science Photo Library/Hank Morgan; 125c Shutterstock; 125b Science Photo
Library/Oscar Burriel; 126tr Shutterstock; 126cr Alamy/Picture Contact BV; 127 Getty Images/AFP; 130, 131 Shutterstock;
135tl Photolibrary/Peter Arnold; 135tr, 135cl, 136, 137, 139t Shutterstock; 139c Science Photo Library/Michael Donne/
University of Manchester; 140t, 140b, 141l Shutterstock; 141r Alamy/Clarke Brennan; 142, 143t, 143b Shutterstock;
144 Alamy/Ashley Cooper; 145r, 146, 147, 148c, 148r, 149l, 149br, 150l, 150r, 152, 153tl, 153l, 153r Shutterstock

The publisher would also like to thank the following illustrators from Linden Artists:
Adam Hook, Stuart Lafford, Patricia Ludlow, Shane Marsh, Sebastian Quigley, Sam Weston

All Creative Corner illustrations by Ray Bryant

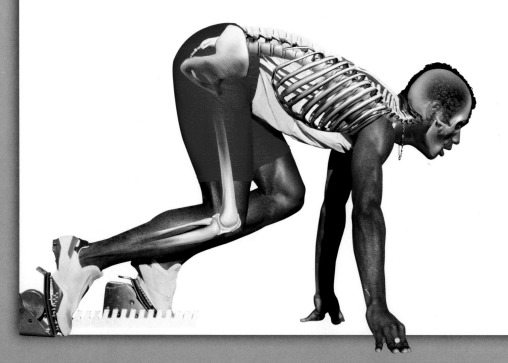